A Patriot's Guide
To Right-Wing Thinking
By Tex Shelters
(aka Joe Callahan)

Baker Street Press
Tucson, Arizona

Published by Baker Street Press
P.O. Box 13866
Tucson, AZ 85732-3866

© 2008 Joe Callahan
All rights reserved. Published 2008.
Printed in the United States of America
ISBN 978-0-9818985-0-6

The Tex Shelters character is too big to be based on only one person. Tex Shelters is an amalgam of many different real life characters and the similarity to any real life person is not coincidental.

The Tex Shelters character and alias is owned by Joe Callahan. Accept no imitations.

This book is dedicated to Ronald Reagan, Joseph McCarthy, Ann Coulter, Michael Savage, Bill O'Reilly, William Dobson, David Horowitz, and all the other great leaders of our patriotic movement to take back America for true Americans.

Cover, Chapter title photos, and other photos of Tex Shelters were taken in Tucson, Arizona by Heidi MacDonald.

All other art created by Joe Callahan unless otherwise cited.

Table of malContents

Preface: A Patriotic Story about the Truth	1
Introduction: The Benefits of Right-Wing Thinking	3
I. Be Afraid; Be Very Afraid	7
II. The Liberal Juggernaut	35
III. Why you're Poor, and Why it's Your Fault	50
IV. God is Our Copilot	70
V. Corporations Should Run Everything	88
VI. Democracy is Our Number One Export	118
Epilogue: How Right-Wing Thinking is Right	143

April,
Keep writing and keep America great!
Tex Shelters

Preface: A Patriotic Story of Truth

This book is about the Right in America and the truth we spread through our leadership. The truth comes in three colors: red, white, and blue. Truth is patriotic and patriotism is truth. <u>A Patriot's Guide to Right-Wing Thinking</u> has all the information in it that you need to be a good American. The stories in this book go beyond the facts. They unveil a deeper truth.

The conservatives in America are the purveyors of morality. Just ask Ann Coulter, author of <u>How to Talk to a Liberal</u> and many other good books that call liberals names. Why bother talking to liberals or learning anything about them when you already know the truth. She tells us that liberals are liars, traitors, rapists, and atheist baby killers. She says it as often as she can in order to prove that it's true.

Coulter and her patriot friends and followers repeat the truths promoted by our leaders in the past. These include such patriots as Nathan Bedford Forrest, Joseph McCarthy, George Wallace, Henry Kissinger, Ronald Reagan, George Bush Sr. and Jr., and Bill O'Reilly. She even repeats the truths she writes in one book in the next book. She is the present day leader in disseminating our message. That's what makes the right wing so strong; we stick to the truth we created.

The President speaks on the radio and television, and this conveys truth. He makes assertions about things based on what he wants us to think, and so do our radio and television allies, our corporate friends, and Congress. This lets Americans know what to believe.

Rush Limbaugh is quite good at this as is Michael Savage. Limbaugh once proclaimed, "Feminism was established so as to allow unattractive women easier access to the mainstream of society" (Media Matters 1). This is true because there are so many Republican voters who dislike uppity women. It supports the manly fact that all women should stay in the home, support the family, and stop complaining.

When talking about prisoner treatment, Michael Savage announced, "Use ... [l]ittle, ugly women. And let 'em take big strapping Iraqis and put 'em on leashes naked" (Media Matters 2). This statement not only makes women in our team happy, but it gives patriots a nice revenge scenario of naked prisoners to visualize.

Statements such as these make our base of voters happy. What we say fits nicely into the long held back-story promoted by the American government, corporations, and our wealthy forefathers. May our truth stand alongside our flag as it waves and defends America around the globe.

If you want to tell the truth, follow the lead of the patriotic right in this country and you too will be believed. All you have to do to demonstrate the truth of your message is to shout loudly when you speak. There is nothing like volume to convey the truth. You can also repeat your message until it becomes true. The more often you say something like "we are promoting democracy in the Middle East", the truer it is.

To defend America, motherhood, families, the flag and the President, buy my book.

Tex Shelters,
from an undisclosed location
December 2, 2007

Introduction: The Benefits of Right-Wing Thinking

Reagan is the father of modern American conservatism. Reagan was a good actor and could show the Americans he was for law and order. He did, for example, play a criminal in the movie *The Killers*. Reagan made it okay to think those patriotic American thoughts that Nixon felt guilty about and Kissinger was demonized for. These thoughts include that the poor are lazy, pollution isn't a problem, we support democracy in the world, stem cells are sacred, tax cuts are always good, and others I share in this book. Reagan made it okay to be a white male in America again.

Our actions in the quest for profits make us great. America lets those who know best control the security and economy of the United States. We are wealthier and safer due to our exportation of democracy and control of resources here and abroad. With the help of the government, the conservatives, the moderates, so-called liberals, the mass media like Fox News, and most of all, the people of America, the rich are getting richer in the United States. Everyone else must be as well.

Politically, we get what we ask for. The public can stick to arguing things they know about such as gay marriage, abortion, and prayer in schools. We talk about weapons of mass destruction (WMDs) to protect America, we talk about swift boats to keep that dangerous liberal John Kerry out of the White House, and we tell you we support whatever you support. We do it for the good of the country.

We care so much about the country that we make more money than the rest of you. Wealth consolidation has made us the world's number one democracy. Because of our rational decision-making, we distribute our wealth to benefit our great nation. There were times (progressive movement, the new deal, civil rights movement, hippyism) when the poor and middle classes were angry and restless about the excesses of the rich. All this envy and hate did for them was to make them look like the unpatriotic liberals that they are.

If you're not rich, you understand that it is your fault *or* the fault of the liberal conspiracy. If you struggle, it's because taxes are too high, or the Constitution is holding you down. People around the world are jealous of us, and they want what we have. Immigrants are stealing from us.

The more truth we tell, the more we enjoy the fruits of life. We conservatives, through our government mouthpieces, have told the truth so long that what we say goes unquestioned. Constructing the truth takes time and resources, resources that only corporations and the Bush led government can afford. From the time of the founding fathers, the patriotic truth has come from the conservative elements of society.

The Beginning of the Right: the Constitution

The wise and benevolent Colonial leaders wrote a constitution. It was written to allow the best bred to rule. Unfortunately, some liberals wanted the Constitution to contain some rights. They whined and whined until we told them we would put in the Bill of Rights. It was the start of the ongoing struggle between the liberals and the Right.

The elite Colonists wrote The Bill of Rights to protect freedoms for everyone; however, only the best people in society could afford those freedoms. The elites owned the printing presses in the 1790s, and that allowed them to say what they wanted. The First Amendment gave the wealthy a protected right to speech and the right to talk to the largest amount of people through the media they owned. Yes, the poor can yell their viewpoints from the street corner, but they will look like the lunatics that they are.

Freedom of speech, religion, press, and assembly are good to have. We just had to make sure that the worthy, the best bred and the elite, could control what people heard. The right wing recognized that the rich knew how to run things better than the poor masses. The courts were packed with our friends to make sure the rights wouldn't get out of control. It's called checks and balances. The Executive Branch and the courts had to check the rights that Congress gave the people.

The Constitution was also written to protect America from losing what they had taken from the natives since the colonization and what they had consolidated in the revolution. It was written to make sure that:

- You had to be well indoctrinated in costly disciplines such as law in order to become an elected or appointed official in the United States.
- You had to have lots of leisure time to run for office, which meant you were rich.
- Having rich friends will ensure you get elected through "free" press coverage and endorsements.
- Voting would be limited to white males so privilege could be maintained.

You see, the particulars have changed, but the formula is the same. Conservatives and their well-endowed allies controlled the power through control of money and media then, and Billionaires do it that way now. That meant the best would rule and the country became great because of it.

The Right Thinking in This Book

People all over the world are out to get us. The government and mass media make sure we know what to be afraid of as a service to the American people. Chapter 1 explains how fear is the only way to keep America the best country in the world. We do our best keeping fear high through our unified message. Alternating fear and hope is a great formula for our continued rule of the nation. A war now and then helps keep the fear high. Liberals just don't understand this. To get on with your distrust and scorn of the left, read chapter 2.

Liberals are the most intolerant people in the world. Ignorance, laziness, and selfishness are the causes of this intolerance. This intolerance leads liberals to make decisions that hurt America. They may believe in rights for gays, immigrants, and raped women who want an abortion, but that just shows how intolerant they are. We have taught America how intolerant liberals are through the news segments our media presents about intolerant liberals. Liberals should be feared and despised. If you don't hate liberals, you hate America and you support the terrorists. You also remain poor if you're liberal. Chapter 3 clarifies this for you.

Poverty is the fault of the poor. Despite all the tax cuts Fortune 500 companies get to create jobs, people are still unemployed. If you're still poor in this climate, in the richest country in the world, you're not working enough jobs. Besides, those immigrants are taking your jobs, so you must support more politicians that talk out against immigration. Republicans aren't poor, so become one of them. In fact, if you truly believed in our God, you wouldn't be poor or at least you wouldn't mind. Being poor would just bring you closer to God and Jesus. I explain this in chapter 4.

The Right is the Godliest group in this country, not matter what we do. God guides us so we can guide America. We are on a crusade to purify this nation and the world. If we make some money along the way, it is God's will. We do whatever it takes to make this country great because we believe in His divine guidance. I prove that in this book. It is by God's will that corporations should rule everything. I explain this in chapter 5.

The United States only exists because corporations exist. They know how to make money, so they should rule our nation. Unpatriotic Americans think the masses should have a say. This hate of corporations is what liberals do because they want socialists to take over our nation. Public education, public health care, and public elections just hurt this country. Corporations know how to make these things great. Corporations know how to create democracy, and they're good at exporting things. That is why we export more democracy every year than any other country. Chapter 6 explains this so that even liberals understand.

Democracy is made great by allowing the Right to rule. Corporations make democracy, and our government exports it for us. We hire corporations like *Blackwater* and *Kellogg, Brown and Root* to reinforce our democracy overseas. We have the greatest tools for democracy in history. We use these tools to make sure people don't hurt us, and thus we remain democratic. These exports also happen to make us some money. With God, democracy, and trade on our side, we will remain the most democratic country in history.

Defending America

The best thing you can do to defend America is to read this book. All you need to know about our great nation and the dangers we face is contained between its pages. This book adds to the great literature on the Right. Like books by Savage, Coulter, O'Reilly, and Joseph Lieberman, A Patriot's Guide to Right-Wing Thinking proves again that we are the best people in the best country in the world.

Chapter I

Be Afraid; Be Very Afraid

Fear is an essential part of becoming a great nation. The most powerful empires in history have utilized fear to become, and stay, powerful. How we manage fear determines whether we will be a mediocre society or a great one. The United States, for instance, is a very fearful country, and we're number one because of our success creating fear. Two other modern examples of great fear based societies are Germany and Japan.

Japan and Germany were very fearful countries that challenged the content nations like England, France, and China for world dominance. The latter countries had very little fear before World War II. Without fear, Japan and Germany would have remained weak. How else can you explain a small island nation in *Asia* becoming so powerful and Germany coming back from the ruins of WWI?

The Japanese and Germans both had large countries, China and the Soviet Union respectively, to fear and despise in the 1930s. They both had nations of people to fear and scapegoat, the Chinese and the Jews. This helped them be great. Their fear propelled them ahead against overwhelming odds.

Today the United States has gays, migrants, the homeless, Arabs, and others to fear and keep us great. On the other boot, to coin a phrase, peaceful Tibetans and Native Americas were conquered because they were too close to the calming powers of nature. Only when China, under Mao Zedong, cast off the blanket of Buddhism did it start to become fearful and great.

Mao Zedong, great fear creating leader of China from 1949-1976, has a special display in the *Fear Hall of Fame*^{TM} for promoting fear at home and abroad. He, along with Stalin, jump-started the Cold War and kept the United States in fear, and thus, kept us great.

I start with fear because when there's a good level of fear, *we all* (Billionaires and politicians) can get *you all* (the people) to act in the nation's self-interest. Fear is the basis for the ways we run things. If we have to exaggerate a little to get you to fear the right things, that's okay.

There is good productive fear I call "political fear" that helps the rich and powerful get on with the running of America with minimal interference, and there is evil fear or "rational fear" that doesn't add to our power and wealth. Being afraid of terrorists, Y2K, and immigrants is good for us, and it's good for America. Fear gives us power and makes us money. Being afraid of losing your job, decreasing world oil reserves, global warming, or inflation is just counter-productive and a waste of time. These fears are just too "rational" to be productive. Let us experts worry about what you should fear.

Corey Robin (<u>Fear: The History of a Political Idea</u>) writes about political fear. Political fear comes from the state and it is our job, and especially the Billionaires, to make sure that personal fears are politicized for the good of the country. As Professor Robin points out, political fear can take at least four levels of intensity: fear, anxiety, terror, and total terror. These levels are akin to the Homeland Security Alert levels, and it is the job of every American to elevate fear as high as possible so that we feel safe. Go to the website to see what the current threat level is (US Terror Alert System: US.gov 2). Here's some information from that site:

> Don't Be Afraid, Be Ready
>
> The Department of Homeland Security's *Ready Campaign* seeks to help American families be better prepared for even unlikely emergency scenarios. We know from intelligence reports that terrorists are working hard to obtain biological, chemical, and radiological weapons, and the threat of attack is real. One of the primary mandates of the Department of Homeland Security is to educate the public, on a continuing basis, about how to be prepared in case of a national emergency -- including a possible terrorist attack (Homeland Security).

What Michael Chertoff and friends are really saying is be afraid, be very afraid.

If we (the power elite) are clever enough, personal fears can be used to keep Americans from fearing Republicans, Neocons and corporations, then we can concentrate on important things like celebrity babies and American Idols. Examples of these "good fears" talked about in the media to make sure you focus on them include the following: fear of identity theft, car jacking, natural disasters, viruses, random killers, and obesity. By constantly telling the public what to fear, we can sell more computer software and credit card insurance, clubs and car alarms, life and health insurance, and more diet pills. Fear keeps this economy humming in many ways. Without fear, we'd be a squirrel without its nuts in winter.

Billionaires and their politicians have helped increase fear over the years and have told the American people what to be scared of as a service to our great country. Because we have not been through the constant terrorist attacks of Europe and the Middle East, and we have not had the modern civil wars of

Africa and Central America, we have had to work hard to create fear. We must be constantly vigilant to ensure that fear stays out of control in America.

The mass media in the United States gives airtime to celebrities and politicians. We listen when the President talks about WMDs, boat attacks, Pearl Harbor, and Iraq. His patriotic message is repeated on every news channel for our benefit. When President Bush talks about Islamo-terrorists, the axis of evil, and anthrax, he is doing his best to keep us afraid and strong.

The events of September 11, 2001 made our job easier. Fear didn't start or end on that day. It was our job, with the help of the White House and all its accomplices, to make the most of that fearful situation, to give it fuel, make it last, and exploit it. No comfort or hope was to be given after 9/11, just anger, terrorist alerts and fear.

Philosophers (damn intellectuals!) have pointed out over the years that fear is an essential motivator (ibid). We need fear. In <u>Democracy in America</u>, Alexis De Tocqueville argues that fear must be used in the cause of liberty. I disagree. We must use fear to get the American people to do what is best for the country regardless of the cost to liberty. Fear can be exaggerated, and politicians and other elite tell their stories in order to increase the fear Americans feel. If we have to exaggerate the dangers of avian flu, talk about putting duct tape on your window because of anthrax spores, or announce an increase in homeland security alerts, we will.

Barry Glassner (<u>The Culture of Fear</u>) suggests that we perceive socially undesirable outcomes such as a disaster in America and come up with politically convenient reasons for these events. The reasons often involve fear of the unknown or outsiders. For example, if the economy takes a downturn, it's the fault of immigrants, never government policies. If divorce rates go up, it's because of gay marriage. If someone is shot, it's the victim's fault for not carrying a gun. We ignore the underlying causes of our problems, or displace our anger to more convenient targets such as gays, non-citizens, poor people, the unemployed, women, minorities, and weak countries overseas. We employ these techniques for the good of the country.

Addressing the real cause of life's downturns such as the concentration of wealth in the hands of corporations and politicians would be dangerous and futile. If we point the fear at constantly changing targets, people will be perpetually afraid, and America will stay strong.

Choosing the Right Objects of Fear

It is the responsibility of every government to choose the correct objects of fear for its citizens. The best fears from a Billionaires standpoint follow:

- A non-threatening weak object of fear, such as a minority group;
- A group that doesn't have regular access to media;
- A hard to point to nebulous kind of object such as the poor, unemployed, and immigrants.

In fact, it is best to fear anything that doesn't link elites to the downturn in the quality of your life. Pointing out how the rich get so much more under President Bush and most administrations would be just class warfare perpetrated by liberals.

We must use of fear to make money and reduce dissent. Fears must create a sense of alert and distraction while not challenging the Billionaires' financial interests. Fears must tap into the subconscious prejudices and have a grain of truth. If I were to talk about fears of alien snakes taking over our brains, *most* of you would laugh at me. On the other hand, fear of a terrorist attack, no matter how unlikely to happen in your town, has a visceral affect on people. Since most immigrants are hard working, fear of immigrants taking away our jobs can be easily instilled in the public. The illness of the month is also a nice fear; all of us have been sick at one point in time and the experience is often very vivid to us. Remember SARS?

Any stranger or unfamiliar group also makes us afraid, so make sure to suspect your neighbor. We need to fear clowns, bombs, migrant workers, identity theft, Arab boys with guns in a far away land we've never heard of, meteors, missiles, viruses, anthrax, and things people tell us to fear.

Billionaires would be afraid of everyone if they weren't so darn busy making sure that the working classes were afraid of each other. If you're White, make sure that you are afraid of Blacks and Latinos. Asians could be feared, but they should definitely be envied and mistrusted. If you're straight, you *must* fear homosexuals. *They* are the cause of so many social ills. Blacks should fear Whites, Latinos and immigrants. Asians should fear other Asians; Latinos need to fear Whites and so on. When the fear and hatred of Arabs and immigrants doesn't work, feel free to despise and fear each other. Like I said, everyone is out to get us.

If you are unclear about what fear level each group should elicit in you, please look at the Fear-o-Matic on the next page. In the graphic, larger lines indicate higher fear levels. The center columns feature major groups in the United States and lines are connecting those to groups they must fear on the outer level. Remember, fear leads to hate, so don't forget to scorn your neighbor this week. It's the Christian thing to do.

A Patriot's Guide to Right-Wing Thinking

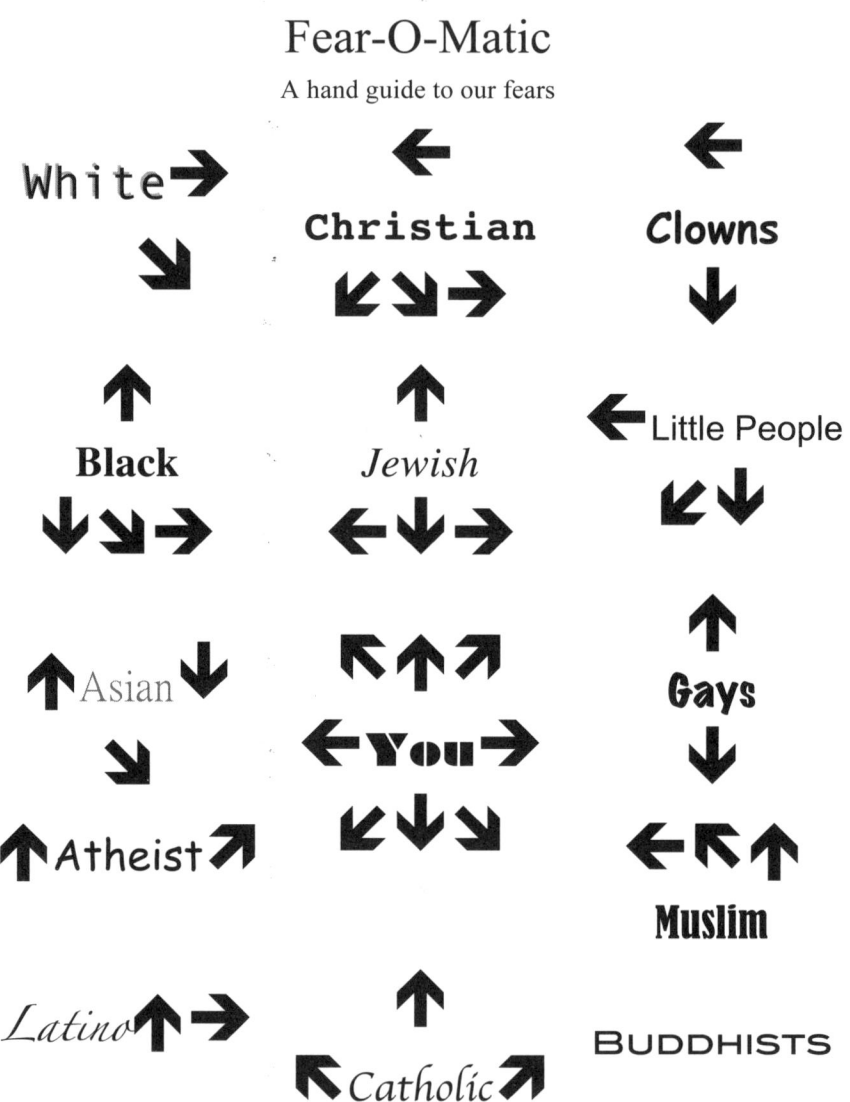

The media must portray external non-relevant fears, fears of events that are unlikely or will never occur, with vivid graphics and exciting language. Seeing is believing, so the more these events are rerun in the media, the more real they are to us. Increased consumption of TV news magazines, COPS, Americas Most Wanted, When Animals Attack, Top Ten Worst Plane Accidents in History and other sensational programming is indicated to create a well-informed, fearful America.

If we can broadcast disasters and runaway brides, a beautiful missing blonde or cute kid, we can do our deals in the back rooms such as cutting veteran's benefits and school lunch programs without notice. We must use words such as "extreme danger," "a new threat," "increased panic," "eminent danger," "right around the corner," "increased cases" and other catchy phrases to increase fear. The potential of fear knows no bounds. Fear keeps us great.

How to begin fear and end questioning

There are two fronts in the war to create fear: the politicians and the mass media. Buying up all the politicians in America streamlines the legislative process and helps us keep the fear coming while we put on our caring faces. Monopolizing media helps us provide better information about what Americans need to fear.

Neocons like to assist the 535 members of Congress by lobbying them and teaching them what to do. We take care of the funding for their campaigns, so they can get to work. We also write legislation using our research institutes to help Congress make laws. That's not even counting the help we Billionaires give the President year in and year out.

There are a few people in Congress, like that pesky Dennis Kucinich and stubborn John Conyers, who try to stir up some solutions. With every whine from their filthy unpatriotic mouths they give aid and comfort to the terrorists. If one person fights back out of the 535 members in Congress, it demonstrates that there really *is* a loyal opposition. If the White House leads with a story, say about WMDs in Iraq, the media presents it as fact at the alter of truth, your television. Then the people believe. Amen!

Even as I write this from my quiet mansion in an undisclosed location, the terror alert system says "elevated" or yellow. I'm wondering, of what, should I be afraid? Fear something damn it, anything, for America, for the flag, be afraid! It's your patriotic duty! By now the American people have bought the terror alert package, and I, Tex Shelters, own a piece of that pie that was sold to you. Thanks for keeping America great by remaining afraid.

Fear and the Creation of Great Empires

Fear has been instrumental in the rise of many great civilizations. Moreover, great civilizations have diminished or collapsed over the years when they stopped tending to their fear. Greek, Roman, Mayan, Aztec, English, and Spanish civilizations all rose and fell based on how well or poorly they tended to their fear.

The British had lots to fear in the early days. First, they had each other. Then there was the succession of invading nations including the Saxons, Norse, Danes, Romans, Normans, and Saxons. France lived right across the *"English* Channel" from England. Notice it's not called the "French Channel." Being invaded by a bunch of stinky non-bathing French folk put so much fear in the British that they had to run to the four corners of the planet just to get away from the stench. By 1921, Britain controlled about 400 million folk, and the empire covered more than 20% of the world's total land area (Microsoft, Encarta Online Encyclopedia). The British had strange people to fear everywhere they went.

After WWII and the British victory (actually ours) over the Nazis, they figured they had nothing left to fear. The British sat on their crumpets sipping tea as their empire withered away. We on the other hand had the Soviets to fear, so we continued being great. It didn't take much to keep that fear going for almost 50 years.

As many leaders have shown over the years, governments rule by fear. Now some people could ask, as a leader, would you rather be feared or loved? That's the wrong question. It's whom you get to love you and whom you get to fear you that is important. As long as you have a few people who love you that are willing to beat the people who fear you into submission, you're all set. That's how we get citizens to do what's best for the nation.

Obviously, some nations are better at creating fear than others. What makes the United States the greatest nation ever is that we're the best storytellers and can create the greatest amount of fear out of the smallest danger.

The United States: A History of Fear

The United States is the greatest country ever because we have the most fearful people. We have had our down times when things got out of control and the people didn't have their fear in hand, but we've always bounced back one way or another. That's the resiliency of the American people and our government. Just when you think it's over for America, a new fear arises and life is good again. From humble beginnings to the world's greatest superpower, we have been blessed by fear and a government that knows how to use fear to its advantage.

The British government in the New World had a well-established relationship with fear in the mid 18th century. Not only was the New World inhabited by savage Indians all out to kill the Colonists, the French were also stinking up North America from Quebec to Louisiana.

As for the Indians, the trickiest were the ones that acted all friendly to the Colonists by helping the Colonists survive. The first Thanksgiving in 1621 was an attempt by the Indians to make the Pilgrims less fearful and later kill them and eat them like stuffed birds. Thankfully, the British Colonists weren't fooled and killed off the friendly Indians. We now call the holiday "Thanksgiving" because we're thankful the Indians didn't fool us and eat us.

The Pilgrims and other English settlers needed to take the land from the Indians in order to have a place to farm and to make a profit. God had, after all, commanded the Pilgrims to move there and take the land. The Colonial leaders had to create a fear of the natives. It wasn't hard to create animosity between Natives and the Colonists. Once the Colonists learned the Indians had no God and wore strange clothing made from the earth in an environmentally sustainable manner, they feared and despised the Indians.

The Colonial governors had a clever plan to start a perpetual war with the natives. They ordered the Colonists to settle as close as possible to Indian villages. These incursions angered the Indians who dared to defend their land against the Colonists. Therefore, the Colonist killed Indians who made them afraid. Americans learned at an early stage of our empire that if you are scared of something, the best thing to do is to destroy it.

The Iroquois were particularly aggressive and created terror in the people in an attempt to remove the Europeans from *our* land in America. After these terrorist attacks by the Iroquois, an English governor told the people, "The Natives attack us because they hate our freedom, they despise our God, and they envy our way of life," and "the Indians are ungrateful for all the help we have given them."

Some of the Colonists thought this was a load of turkey turds, but this reasoning was needed to justify their fear and hatred of the Indians. Most of the Colonists believed that the governor would not lie to them, for he was a man of God. Fear of the Natives had been created and all was going according to God's will.

This fear propelled the Colonists into the frontier to kill the offending Indians. The Indians brought the tragedy upon themselves. If they hadn't been so scary, this might never have happened. Who are we to disagree? Just read the official version that tells us it's the Indians fault that they lost their land and got killed. If you need proof of the dangers the Indians posed, watch more old time westerns.

The End of British Rule

The British rulers spread fear to the Colonists for 150 years before the Americans rose up against them. That is quite an accomplishment. It was just too hard for the British to keep the Colonist afraid of them in the New World when the Spanish were planning to invade England and the French kept up their hateful attacks against the British in Europe. It's no wonder the English were caught unaware and the Colonists took over in the 1780s.

What the British needed to do is turn the Colonial hatred of the them into hatred and fear of the French and recruit the Colonist for a war against their European enemy, "The French want to force you to work in their vineyards and make you eat brie!" they could have said. Fear of the French might have saved the colonies for England by siphoning off young men to fight overseas and focusing the Colonists' energy on Europe instead of problems of unemployment and poverty at home. It's this strategy that got President Bush reelected, didn't it?

The Declaration of Independence (DOI) was a great document for bringing the fear of the English King to all time highs in the Colonies and thus helping start the Revolutionary War. In fact, according to a Colonial Times/New World Press poll at the time, fear of the King rose 25% after the DOI was published. We know polls are never wrong or biased if the White House or I use them.

There's a whole list of grievances against the King in the DOI. Some of the offences are actual quotes from the Declaration of Independence with commentary on what Jefferson surely feared when he wrote it:

Declaration: *He has called together legislative bodies at places unusual, uncomfortable, and distant from the depository of their public Records, for the sole purpose of fatiguing them into compliance with his measures.*

Jefferson: The fiend, he is tiring out our Congress! How dare he make our Congress travel and work for their pay!

Declaration: *He has dissolved Representative Houses repeatedly, for opposing with <u>manly firmness</u> his invasions on the rights of the people.* (Underline mine for emphasis).

Jefferson: Without a Congress, the common folk would walk around aimlessly! He attacks us with his "manly firmness!"

Declaration: *He has made Judges dependent on his Will alone, for the tenure of their offices, and the amount and payment of their salaries.*
Jefferson: Judicial activism I tell you!
Declaration: *For Quartering large bodies of armed troops among us.*
Jefferson: How dare one nation put thousands of troops on the soil of a sovereign nation and pretend that it's to protect the people and promote democracy when we know it's just to extract the wealth of that nation! This George is a mad tyrant!
Declaration: *For cutting off our Trade with all parts of the world.*
Jefferson: Free trade for the Colonies, and later, NAFTA!
Declaration: *For imposing Taxes on us without our Consent.*
Jefferson: How dare the King tax the wealthy merchants! Let the commoner pay!
Declaration: *He has plundered our seas, ravaged our Coasts, burnt our towns, and destroyed the lives of our people.*
Jefferson: Listen here my good man, burning and plundering towns and destroying lives is what we do to the Indians, not each other.

The Declaration of Independence set up the structure in which the Colonial merchants would be free from taxes and independent to do what they want. It also created fear and anger of a King and the whole British Empire and set forth the ideology of a revolution.

Revolution and Beyond

In the early days of the United States, England was the most powerful nation in the world and still created a lot of fear. There was the great expanse of North America for the new nation to conquer. We also had the great Indian scourge to increase our fears.

The Indians were always just beyond the next ridge, past the next river, hiding in the woods. The Indians were always trying to hurt the white man and even get a "brother" (as Negros like to be called) now and again. There were also more Africans coming in from Africa in the Colonial times and that was creating a great scare in the South. Overall, the birth of the nation was scarier than real live childbirth without drugs. Thankfully, D. W. Griffith put all that on film in the great documentary Birth of a Nation.

The fight over slavery was horrible. After they had been so well treated on the plantation, those poor slaves were so unceremoniously thrown out into the dirt road without a place to live or a job. Those that didn't die on the journey to America, and the ones that didn't die from overwork or whippings at the hands of the slave owners did pretty well. Luckily for the blacks, the Industrial

Revolution was starting in the North after the Civil War, and there were plenty of jobs up in the North that had many of the features of plantation work: long hours, backbreaking labor, and shacks called tenements where workers lived.

While the former slaves were paid, their pay was the lowest. This made Negroes feel right at home. While the black man would surely miss the wonderful southern hospitality after the Civil War, and he had to put up with all of the immigrants in the North, the Negro did mighty fine to be sure. One former first lady added, "They were poor in the South and are being treated quite well in the North. This slavery thing turned out quite well for them." Funny how Barbara Bush, the Presidents mommy, stole that quote when referring to the evacuees from hurricane Katrina in Houston, "Everyone is so overwhelmed by the hospitality. And so many of the people in the arena here, you know, were underprivileged anyway, so this is working very well for them (Nation Magazine)."

There was a bad time as we tried to get through the reconstruction after the War of Northern aggression that liberals call "The Civil War". Finally, Teddy Roosevelt or William (Randy) Hearst or someone came up with the phrase, "Remember the Maine", and that meant we were afraid of the Spanish. We *had* to attack the Spanish in Cuba, thus starting the Spanish-American War in 1898.

The Maine was a battleship that exploded on February 15, 1898. The navy could never determine the cause of the explosion, and many experts assumed it was an accident. Nevertheless, newspaper mogul William Randolph Hearst accused Spain of an attack in his papers and other newspapers followed. The cry "Remember the Maine" was used to get the United States into a profitable war. We invaded Cuba with the help of President Roosevelt (the kooky Teddy, not the commie cousin Franklin), grabbed some other Spanish properties such as Puerto Rico, Guam, and the Philippines, and took our rightful place as a world power.

When we took over, we guaranteed independence for these islanders and backed dictators who would let us extract well-earned profits from the former Spanish properties. We also let the dictators take their share from our profits for running things for us. What we explained to the American people was that we did it for freedom and democracy. We did it to keep America rich.

A lot if immigrants came to the United States between 1880 and 1910. The continued immigration from overseas was needed so we could fear foreigners. This helped workers right here at home be grateful for all of the hours corporations had been giving them. Luckily for the workers in the early 1900s, work hours could be nearly sixteen hours a day if they were good at what they did. Industrialists were even kind enough to give their children work during the Industrial Revolution, a time of immense factory building and profit making. "Give us your poor tired and huddled masses" is right.

The trick to handling labor is to let enough immigrants in to keep wages low while passing laws to keep some immigrants out. That's why Bush favors a guest worker program, not a permanent citizen amnesty. White rulers targeted Asians for exclusion in the late 1800s because they were scary. The Chinese had the audacity to build the railroad across the country so the white folks could sell more products from sea to shining sea. How dare they!

The Industrial Revolution was a great boon for Americans, entrepreneur and worker alike. Government was in its place, business was under-regulated, and we made a lot of money. We created millions of menial jobs to help the people and improved the infrastructure of this great nation. The railroads lead the way to prosperity for everyone. Unfortunately, that meant letting in more Irish and Chinese immigrants. About 2,300 Chinese were hired in the 1860s at approximately twenty-eight dollars per month to do the dangerous work of building the railroads through the Sierra Mountains from the west coast and into the Great Plains (Central Pacific Railroad Photographic History Museum).

Today we have a problem with Mexicans coming over to take our jobs. No matter what we do to make them feel unwelcome, they keep coming. Just because their government won't help people survive in Mexico doesn't mean we're responsible for them. We do what we can to send them our assembly jobs in the border factories. You think they would be grateful and stay on their side of the border.

What happened after we beat the Spanish in 1898 is we ran out of enemies for a while. We could always count on the immigrants, who came in droves from Europe, to kick up fear. Moreover, all those race riots against blacks and immigrants for taking jobs away from honest white folks kept us in fear. When unions started making headway in the 1900s, and those damn progressives got in the way of progress. We had to use Pinkertons and other strikebreakers to stop those anti-American unionists.

The Pinkertons were a band of patriots who protected factories from communists by beating up, and sometimes killing, workers who wanted higher wages. What good would it be for the workers if we shut down the factories? All this fear kept this nation on a course to be numero uno.

People started loosing their fear of the elite and of other countries in the early 1900s, women felt some liberation, "flapped around," and they got the right to vote with the Nineteenth Amendment in 1920. Women getting the vote lead directly to the Great Depression in 1929. Don't let them liberals tell you that over-speculation in the stock market, global reductions in demand for United States goods, over production of manufactured goods and farm products, and increased personal debt caused the depression. With more people (women) able to vote, people got too optimistic, and everything turned rotten.

They eat babies, don't they?

In 1917 Woodrow Wilson, a good Democrat if there is such a thing, had to get the public all revved up for war against the Germans. The problem is that his 1916 re-election slogan was, "He kept us out of war." Something had to be done in the wake of growing socialism in the U.S.A.

Socialism would mean people from different countries would work together for a common cause, and that couldn't be good. Working together is downright un-American. It is every man for him. Social Darwinism, survival of the fittest, helped the aristocracy know they were better adapted to the climate and life on earth. Our riches prove we are better adapted.

To get us to join WWI, we had to get everyone to fear the Germans. Focusing only on the atrocities the Germans were committing in Europe with the use of submarines and mustard gas made us fear the Krauts. Never mind that the British and French were committing their own atrocities, like using submarines and mustard gas.

The cure for rising socialism was, and is today, having the poor and working classes (possible socialist recruits) join the military to fight against a common enemy. In 1917, it was Germany. Nationalism, extreme love of country, can be used as a recruiting tool. The poor defend the property and investments of the wealthy classes, thus protecting our American way of life. In addition, the patriotic American industries were willing to open up their factories to make weapons for the war effort while only taking a tiny profit. Look at the table on the next page featuring the pre-war vs. intra-war profits for American companies involved in World War I.

After telling the American people the U.S. wouldn't enter into the profitable war in Europe, President Wilson started the Committee on Public Information. The goal of the committee was to convince the people that war was for their own good and the good of America. The committee sponsored 75,000 speakers who gave 750,000 four-minute speeches in five thousand cities and towns to make the argument against the Germans and for entry into WWI (Zinn 355).

U.S. Corporate Profits during WWI

Company	Average profits in the last pre-war year	Average profits during the four years of the war
U. S. Steel	$105,331,000	$259,653,000
Du Pont	$6,092,000	$58,076,000
Bethlehem Steel	$6,840,000	$49,427,000
Anaconda Copper	$10,649,000	$34,549,000
Utah Copper	$5,776,000	$21,622,000
American Smelting	$11,566,000	$18,602,000
Republic Iron and Steel	$4,177,000	$17,548,000
International Mercantile	$6,690,00	$14,229,000
Atlas Powder	$485,000	$2,374,000
American and British Man.	$172,000	$325,000
Canadian Car & Foundry	$1,335,000	$2,201,000
Crocker Wheeler	$206,000	$666,000
Hercules Powder	$1,271,000	$7,430,000
Niles, Bement Pond	$656,000	$6,146,000
Scovill Mfg. Co.	$655,000	$7,678,000
General Motors	$6,954,000	$21,700,000

(Price)

The tendency of new German immigrants to live in cultural enclaves apart from other ethnic groups in the United States made them an easy target of suspicion that created fear. In addition, some brilliant propagandist started calling the Germans "Huns", meaning *uncontrolled destructive people*. We certainly must be against Germany because we're anti-Hun in America, and we knew Germans were Huns because someone told us so.

Today we have the Patriot Act to create suspicion of each other and Wilson, along with a majority *Democratic* Congress, passed the *Espionage Act* in June 1917 to do the same thing. The *Espionage Act* didn't stop foreign spies in America like Wilson said it would. The law made it a crime to use free speech to say things that might undermine our war operations. The *Espionage Act* provided twenty years in prison for "'Whoever, when the United States is at war, shall willfully cause or attempt to cause insubordinations, disloyalty, mutiny, or refusal of duty in the military or naval forces of the United States, or shall willfully obstruct the recruiting or enlistment service of the United States...(Zinn 356).'" Congress extended this act just like the Patriot Act! We need to bring this law back to prevent people from abusing their free speech outside of military recruiting offices during protests. What good is free speech if we can't arrest people for using it?

The *Espionage Act* worked. In 1917, two months after the law was passed, they nabbed Charles Schenck for sending out *pamphlets* that denounced the draft and WWI. He was obstructing the war effort by making *pamphlets* and should have gotten more than six months in jail for what he did. By the time he got out, the United States had its troops overseas winning the Great War for liberty. The greatest thing about these arrests was that it created real fear in anarchists and socialists, so the smart traitors kept their mouths shut out of fear. Now do you believe me when I say fear keeps us great?

World War II: Perfecting Fear

Even though we disliked and feared the Germans still from WWI, and they had turned Nazi, the American public just didn't want to do their patriotic duty and go to Europe to be killed by Germans again. The Nazis were only slaughtering Jews, and the American press and White House didn't feel killing Jews was news.

In 1938, a law-breaking shipload of German Jewish refugees aboard the SS St. Louis was trying to get into United States waters just because some of them were being persecuted and killed in Europe. It wasn't our mess to clean up. Therefore, President Roosevelt turned them away from our bases in Cuba, and they were not permitted to dock in the United States. That is the way it should be. Laws should be followed no matter who is being hurt, because the law's the law. It's best to ignore bad news like the Darfur refugee crisis in Africa and Jews dying in Europe and stay the course. Besides, the press has celebrities to follow.

We didn't want to invade Europe while American corporations were making millions supplying arms to England and the Allies as well as financing Nazi Germany at the start of Hitler's rise to power in the 30s. Some liberal traitors want to give away top-secret information and tell us about how Prescott Bush, the President's granddad, helped the Nazis with funding for their war effort and reconstruction (Buchanan and Michael). Big deal! There was profit to be made, and we all know that profit comes first! All we had to do was ignore a few atrocities while we made money off the war. If Europe was a no go for war because it was only Jews being killed and countries with names like "Czechoslovakia" being invaded, Asia was a different story.

Asian countries weren't taking out loans or buying our weapons like Europe was, so why not attack them. The problem was getting the U.S. excited about attacking Japan when it was just one Asian group of Evil Japs attacking another Asian people, the honorable Chinese. How we could tell the Japanese from the Chinese and Koreans, I'll never know.

We started provoking the Japanese by giving the Chinese free planes, training them to kill the Japanese, and cutting off Japanese oil, but they just wouldn't attack us. What we needed to do was let them have a strategic target, say Pearl Harbor, which they could attack. Once that happened, we could be afraid of them and go in for the kill.

On October 7, 1940, Lieutenant Commander Arthur H. McCollum, head of the Office of Naval Intelligence and Jap expert, wrote a memo about how, in just eight easy steps, we could get Japan to attack us. That's kind of like provoking your little brother to hit you so you can pound him into the ground. Lt. McCollum told us we should cut off their oil, arm the Chinese, take away access to

---

Freedom Foods

Spanish-American War
Paella becomes "Revolution Rice" in honor of the Cuban Independence fighters

*World War I
Frankfurters turn into "Liberty Sausage" and Sauerkraut becomes "Liberty Cabbage"

World War II
Sake becomes "Drink of Chinese Independence"

Cold War
Borscht becomes "Polish Solidarity Soup" Vodka becomes "Victory Gin"

*Iraq War II
French fries become "Freedom Fries"

*These are true.

Indonesian rubber, cut off food, and so on. Then Japan would attack the United States.

President Franklin D. Roosevelt, while being sympathetic to commies, was no dummy. By the time that Japan finally attacked the United States at Pearl Harbor on December 7, 1941, Roosevelt had done just what that brilliant Lieutenant McCullum said to do (Stinnett). Thank God Japan finally got the message and attacked the United States. Setting up Japan for attack made us the most powerful country in the world. It was, after all, their fault for being born on a small island and daring to try to have *Monroe Doctrine* like control of Asia.

If you don't know, the *Monroe Doctrine* was a statement by the wise and powerful President James Monroe to Congress, but really Europe. It told Europe to "get your hand out of our back yard, America, and we won't covet your back yard, Europe". That's how we got to run things in Central and South America without interference.

The Red Scare: Keeping America Strong

The greatest boon to modern political fear in United States history, even greater than terrorism, is the second red scare. Thanks to the Soviet Union, China, Korea, Cuba, Vietnam and other commies here and abroad, we've had something to be scared of for over ninety years. Being scared of communism helped keep America's eyes on the prize: controlling everything so we can make the world a better place.

The United States was able to use communism to create fear. Fear was necessary to take action and control areas of the world that we would have had a hard time justifying in the past. Therefore, the fear of communism was a win-win situation. We won because we gained influence over much of the third world, and the third world benefited from this influence.

The benefits of exaggerating the fears of communism throughout the years are immeasurable. We had the first Red Scare from 1910-1920. The idea was that communists were everywhere. That allowed us to pass the *Espionage Act* and start busting unions. We got to put people in jail and make sure that labor laws were resisted. If we passed labor laws like the eight-hour day, child labor prohibitions or minimum wages, it would have helped communists in America. Helping workers is essentially a communist endeavor.

Russia became the Soviet Union in 1922, and they were scarier than ever after we won WWII for them. We blockaded Eastern Europe and started a nuclear and conventional arms race with the Soviets. The fear we promoted was that the Soviets could take over the world. This fear allowed us to create the biggest arsenal the world has ever known, boost our economy through arms production, and open new markets through show of force. We were so convinced of the truth that we were able to ignore signs of Soviet collapse starting in the 1970s. The Cold War and arms race was a boon for us all.

The red scare number two started at the Yalta conference on the Crimean Sea. President Roosevelt was sick at that 1945 conference and in his wheel chair, and he wasn't on top of things. In a traitorous act that led to the great Cold War, Roosevelt practically gave Stalin the keys to Eastern Europe. Worst of all, Roosevelt didn't have Rumsfeld or Condi to back him up when he made mistakes like our guy has. You see, our guy's smart and has other folks to think for him.

After Roosevelt gave in to Stalin, he died and left the A-bomb droppings and the end of WW II to Truman who, I'm sure, couldn't have been so happy about it. Vice Presidents are supposed to go to funerals, meet with diplomats from countries like Luxemburg and Latvia, and that's about it. There's nothing in the job description for Vice President about "ending wars" or "dropping big bombs on people".

Nevertheless, Truman was up to it. He dropped that bomb, two in fact, on Japan. His efforts led to the greatest money making adventure in world history: the Cold War. Now some of you wonder why Truman dropped the bomb. The best story we have is that the bombing was to save American lives. Truman pulled that number, one million, out of the air. Certainly, we were concerned about American lives, and that's the only part of the A-bomb attack on Japan we need to hear about. We start all the wars, like the Iraq War II, to save American lives.

The United States didn't worry about the number of American lives that would be lost when we sent U.S. soldiers to the beaches of Normandy in France to die trying to kill the Germans. We had to sell the idea that those Japs were tough so we could use nuclear weapons on them. Remember Pearl Harbor? And it was all about saving American lives.

So what if the Soviet Union was planning to attack the Japs on their island on August 8, 1945 (Zinn 414)? We weren't worried about that. We had to bomb the Japs right away to save American lives, not prevent a commie invasion of the islands. However, that was good thinking dropping the big one on Hiroshima on August 6, two days before them Russians got there.

After the war, the Soviets were easy to fear because they kept on occupying Eastern Europe in Poland, Eastern Germany, Czechoslovakia, and Hungary. This created fear in lots of folks and helped keep the American people in line during the Cold War.

In 1949, some Russians stole our A-bomb technology and the nuclear arms race was off. Luckily, 1949 was the same year that Mao took over China. That gave us two huge commie countries to be afraid of instead of one. You had your China, with a billion rice eaters, and The Soviet Union with an A-bomb. That allowed our Congress to pass all sorts of legislation against commie actors, unionists, intellectuals, the loyal opposition, and anyone who went to parades and picnics with any of the above. America stayed strong and free by threatening to tell stories about people's past lives as communists.

The United States had been supporting the honest and noble Chiang Kai-Shek in China with weapons and training to fight the communists. The fall of China to communists created a breeding ground for communism and fear for years to come.

Chiang Kai-Shek did his best by killing anyone he suspected of being communist or supporting communists. Despite all the killing, detentions, and torture, the ungrateful population rose up against Chiang and became communist. The good part was that the United States could now intervene in Southeast Asia using communist China as a justification. Thus, we could spread more democracy through military occupation like we do in Iraq today.

Korea was the next great battleground between the free world and communism. We invaded Korea because the north was turning communist. We got to spend millions of dollars on bombs in the war and created the great car making country of South Korea. We stopped them commies at the 38th (North) Parallel and the rest of Asia was then safe from communists. We had to stop Korea from becoming fully communist in order to prevent the rest of the region from becoming communist. It worked!! And shut up you liberals who think the dictators we put in place were worse than the communists. Nothing is worse than communists are. Just ask the Nazis from Germany.

Because we stopped communism in Asia, the commies had to come to our hemisphere to spread their viral ideology. That means Fidel Castro. He took over Cuba from the benevolent dictator Batista in 1959, and everything went to hell. We've had to blockade Cuba ever since just to keep communism from reaching Miami.

The Soviets were behind the coup in Cuba, even if you read otherwise in some history book or encyclopedia. And don't listen to the liberals about how Castro made diplomatic overtures to the United States after he took over. Why should we listen to someone who hurt our casino-owning, whore-mongering friends in the United States and Cuba?

Vietnam was a different story. We intervened in Vietnam to help our French allies against the Viet Cong, a group of tunnel digging communists. Ho Chi Mihn, the leader of the communists, put hope of a better future into the minds of the easily persuaded country peasants. I don't know what else they needed other than a muddy shack and a bowl of rice a day. So the lazy peasants, under their comrade leader, rose up against the aristocracy and started killing them.

The United States wanted to protect the status quo once again for the rulers and peasantry. We only killed one million Vietnamese, and only 58,000 U.S, soldiers died, but we gave up. If only we had been willing to kill, say, five million Vietnamese, we might have won that war. The embarrassment and fear that war created in our great leaders today have allowed us to invade and stay in Iraq. Let's hope we go all the way this time and clean out Iraq of Islamo-fascists.

The facts are indisputable: we saved millions of lives by going into these commie-loving countries and cleaning out the riff-raff. If we hadn't used fear to motivate the country, this life saving might never have occurred. Thank God we were so afraid of commies that we could go on supporting military dictatorships. See chapter six for more about the United States and friendly dictatorships.

McCarthyism

McCarthyism was a time in the United States, the late 1940s to the late 1950s, of intense patriotism and good feelings. It was a time when we could vilify people we didn't like by calling them communists. We do this today by calling them liberals or *weak on terrorism*. This period, also referred to as the second red scare, is named for its main proponent, Joseph McCarthy. McCarthyism was a great time when people named names and pointed pointers.

One thing I like about McCarthyism is that the fear was so deep, even liberals called it an "anti-communist crusade." That would be like calling ambulance chasing lawyers anti-accident. We needed communism to justify all of the overseas interventions on behalf of United States corporations. How else could we have incurred into countries that wanted to nationalize their land and resources for their people or renege on U.S. bank loans? All we had to do was tell the people that we were intervening to prevent a country from turning communist. After Congress and the people heard that, we were given all the money we needed for the war. That kept our country's banks and corporations strong and profitable.

Many great conservative storytellers of the twentieth century have demonstrated the link between communism and liberalism. Rabid liberals retort by saying that the Soviets didn't practice true Marxist communism and that communism is about sharing resources and such. Because they're communists, liberals even say that they're not commies.

Now, on the surface, McCarthyism was an anti-communist movement. However, it was so much more. The great patriotic Senator Joseph McCarthy of Wisconsin was protecting us from all sorts of dangers. First, there were Presidents Roosevelt and Truman. The reason McCarthy disliked Roosevelt was that the socialist New Deal program created the minimum wage, the eight-hour work day, unemployment insurance, and other harmful things for the American people. In fact, he hated anyone that helped with the New Deal.

McCarthy was also against the ACLU (American Civil Liberties Union). He understood that people in America don't need civil liberties, and that these liberties are a shield for communists. He also liked to attack unions because they protect the rights of workers, thus promoted socialism.

Others he despised included rock and roll musicians with their sex, drugs, and rock and roll. It's just one big party to these communists. He hated gay and lesbian activists. Communism leads people to be gay, and gays are always recruiting. In the same vein, he hated film stars and Hollywood writers because they're democrats and usually gay. Therefore, he was also against the Girl Scouts because they are recruiting grounds for feminists and lesbians.

The fear of communism allowed McCarthy to implicate all sorts of people who disagreed with him. If only he had been given Mao or Stalin like powers, he would have gotten rid of all those questionable people then and there and sent them off to re-education or work camps. Joseph McCarthy created the House Committee on Un-American Activities (HUAC) to enforce his allegations against Americans. He gave Hollywood and Broadway special scrutiny and lots of communists, or at least people accused of *being* communist, lost their jobs. Anti-communism was not just a matter of ideology but also a matter of national security.

If those accused of being commies didn't point the finger at their colleagues and friends, they lost their jobs and many never found work again. Liberals say the accused were innocent. That is just not true. Being accused of being a communist is enough to show how guilty you are.

People were afraid. If you joined a union, you were labeled a communist and could lose your job or be arrested. Union membership went down because people were afraid of being labeled "communist". Unions can negotiate higher wages and benefits, and rising wages and benefits for most workers are communist and bad for the American people. Roosevelt made it popular to unionize when we needed workers during WWII. However, we didn't need so many workers after the war. McCarthyism and the Cold War helped vilify unions to preserve the American dream.

Joseph McCarthy was a true patriot that wasn't afraid to stick his neck out and accuse anyone he disliked of being communist. He knew how to create fear in the critics of America in Hollywood and on Broadway. His patriotism allowed America to increase our military spending and intervene overseas. His righteous paranoia was a model for the fear used in the war on terrorism.

Terrorism: A New Beginning

Thanks to President Ronald Reagan, the Cold War ended in 1991. That was great because it allowed George Bush, Sr. to get elected riding on Reagan's saddle. It also gave our great GOP (God's Only Party) the political saint, Saint Reagan, it really needed.

A national traitor, Richard Pipes (<u>The Fall of Communism: the Last Empire</u>), dares to believe that other factors led to the fall of communism. He says things such as long-term Soviet economic stagnation, the aspirations of the national minorities, and intellectual dissent are the underlying causes of the Soviet collapse. The protracted war in Afghanistan, the Chernobyl nuclear disaster, and Mikhail Gorbachev's inability to keep the Soviet Union together, were the incidental events that hastened the empire's demise.

We know that it was Reagan's indomitable leadership that led to the collapse of the Soviet Union. Why listen to liberals who studied the Soviet Union for years when you can get your facts from people who worship Reagan? Reagan caused the collapse of the Soviet Union, so we had to create terrorism.

The Soviet Union's collapse wasn't completely good for us. What were we to do without the Soviet Union helping increase arms sales and electing "strong on defense" Republicans. We needed a new enemy. That's where terrorism comes in.

Terrorism is an attempt to create fear in populations using violence or threats of violence as a means to control a population and get concessions. Since most people create fear in others, we're all potential terrorists. With terrorism, you don't have to limit your fear to communist nations. In fact, any nation or individual can be a threat to America if we fear terrorism. The Dali

Lama creates fear in the Chinese, so he's a terrorist. Baseball pitchers create fear in opponents, so they're terrorists. Stephen King creates fear, so he's a terrorist. My neighbor's dog is a terrorist because he scares me. Clowns are terrorists because they scare a lot of people.

Terrorists are trying to create fear in the population, and our government is trying to use this terror to get people to live in fear. Thanks for the helping hand, terrorists. Terrorists have helped us pass laws such as FISA and the Patriot Act to control our population because they have created fear we could use to improve this nation.

Reagan was a visionary who saw the future use of terrorism and how it could lead to increased power and wealth for his patrons, the have-mores. He started us on the path toward attacking "terrorist states" by bombing Libya in 1986, and 9/11 brought the war on terrorism to the forefront of our consciousness. Reagan understood that people who use fear against our friends or us are terrorists. However, when the United States uses fear, it is not terrorism. It is democracy.

9/11—A Great Boon for Conservatives

We all know the date 9/11/01. On that day, the Billionaires had a big party to celebrate our good fortune. Bush had just been elected in 2000, and he wasn't as popular as we Billionaires needed him to be. He just had to have a disaster to become popular again. Now I'm not saying he planned it and all. What I'm saying is that it was good for the Bush Team that people were so afraid of terrorism after 9/11, and that Americans wanted to strike out and kill. The people would do anything that Bush wanted and Congress obliged.

What was President George to do after the World Trade Towers collapsed? He had an agenda to help America be great. He wanted so much to be tough and prove to Daddy that he was strong; therefore, he found a strong country to invade, Iraq. The military knew about Iraq from killing there before, and Iraq has oil. What other reasons do you need to invade? However, he had to prove to people that Iraq was a threat. He had to tell the story of WMDs. Let's look at how the stories are told.

Here are the steps to creating fear of a nation or state:
- Choose a credible, unpopular enemy. Iraq is far away, it is not European, and a dictator ran it. Iraq was a perfect target.
- Choose a weak country that can't actually do you harm. The embargo and continuous bombing of Iraq since the first gulf war has kept them weak. We also have spent a lot of time and money demonizing them, so increasing the hatred of Iraq was easy.

- We must choose a country that other countries hate, fear, or distrust. We could easily invade Holland and conquer the clog-hopping inhabitants. However, those Dutchmen are popular in Europe and people might complain if we wanted to take over their wind power generating capacity. People despise and fear Iraq, and there aren't many countries, countries that we care about, that will fight to defend them.
- Attach a fear to that target nation that can't be disproved without the government investigating the accusations that create the fear. For example, Iraq is a terrorist state that has WMDs and helped plan 9/11. Here's how this logic works and makes us great:

    If A= B and B=C then A=C, so

    A. Apes are animals.
    B. Humans are animals.
    C. Apes are humans.

That is clearly not literally true, only figuratively. So, what about Iraq:

A. Terrorists attacked the United States on 9/11.
B. Saddam Hussein is a terrorist (he killed thousands of Iraqi Kurds).
C. Therefore, Saddam Hussein attacked the United States.

Now, don't fret. This logic was very logical. We needed to have more bases in the Middle East, we needed access to oil, so why not Iraq? That way we can remain great! Sure, thousands of Iraqis and United States soldiers might die, but that's the price for freedom right? If you look at a map of the Middle East, Iraq is in a perfect place for us.

Iraq is next to some of the largest oil fields in the world in Saudi Arabia, its periphery countries, and Iran. It puts us within bombing range of Palestine, Russia, Turkish Kurds, Pakistan, India, and China. Not that we don't already have first strike capability, but is doesn't hurt to double up on your bombing capacity and get closer to the target.

Iraq is a great place to invade. They have oil, they are weak, it is right in the middle of pools of oil, lots of countries dislike them, and it creates more enemies to fear and invade later (crossing my fingers). All around, the Iraq adventure has been great for America.

There are other benefits to this war on terrorism. Fear has allowed the government to take many positive steps.

Guantanamo

First, we have Guantanamo and the "indefinite detentions" of "enemy combatants". In 1901, Representative Thomas Platt added an amendment to a congressional army appropriations bill, the Platt Amendment. This gave the

United States a permanent navy base on the island of Cuba that we still control today. Now it is being used to house "enemy combatants" that the justice department has held in unlimited detention since the second war in Iraq started. We are now afraid that detainees we have held there for over a year will become terrorists because of their resentment and we can't let them go. So what if we torture some of them? If the Cubans torture people on the island, why can't we?

Terror Alert System

The Terror Alert System was designed to alert people about when they should be terrorized. The system started right after 9/11 as the Bush Team was planning how to invade Iraq and give some defense contracts to their friends at Halliburton, Flour, Bechtel Group Inc. and other corporate contributors to the Bush-Cheney ticket (Charlie Cray). The Bush Team needed a way to keep the populace in fear of possible terrorism. Thus, we have the terror alert warnings. The media was like a dog in heat waiting for the terror alert level of the day and the White House played them like banjos.

Don't ask where the terror alert system was before 9/11 when it could have been useful to prevent, say, 9/11. We don't need that kind of un-American questioning. We didn't need to know about the war plans for Iraq that were already in place pre-9/11. Thanks to the fear created by 9/11, the United States was able to invade Iraq. Iraqis don't need the oil like we do. Can we help it if the Intelligent Designer made the mistake of putting our oil under their soil?

TIPS

The Terrorism Information and Prevention System (TIPS) encourages citizens to turn each other into the feds if they feel their neighbor is a threat. Just the very idea that your friends and neighbors could turn you in creates fear in the populous ala McCarthyism. This clever idea was announced by former Attorney General John Ashcroft.

Airport security, shoe security

Thanks to the 9/11 hijacking, private security companies were able to sell their services to the FAA (Federal Aviation Administration). More jobs were created and wages could be lowered because you don't need to adhere to the federal minimum wage if you're a private contractor. Moreover, thanks to Richard Reid in 2001 trying blow up an American Airplanes flight with a shoe bomb, we all must take our shoes off at the airport. Sales of slip-on sandals and shoes with Velcro have risen dramatically since 9/11.

With us or against us

I'm sure you're with us, because if you were against us, you wouldn't be reading this book. If you're against us, please turn yourself in to the TIPS hotline immediately. If you're with us, be vigilant! Constant fear of random incarceration has created many a great government: Maoist China, the Soviet Union, Nazi Germany, Chile, and Argentina in the 1980s among others.

With the Patriot Act, we get to spy on you, enter your home without a warrant, and look at what books you buy or what DVDs you watch, and so on. This way, if you rent *Fahrenheit 9/11*, the movie by the traitorous Michael Moore, we know you're dangerous.

In the past, it was the communists. Today, if you're not with us, "you're with the terrorists". Thomas Friedman of the New York Times had a good idea from his July 22, 2005 column; let's create a blacklist of all of those that try to explain the causes of terrorism by writing or talking about the role the U.S. plays in global violence (Fair Action Alert). See, even the liberal New York Times understands that free speech has a price.

Bush gets re-elected

Many people voted for Bush because they were afraid of what a Democrat like that liberal Kerry would do if elected. There was no need to improve the situation in Iraq. Hey, Bush started it, so we should let him finish. Let's say someone was smashing my neighbor's car with a sledgehammer. I would certainly let him finish the job because I know the car would work better after the smashing. That's just like Iraq. Bush started this deconstruction project in Iraq, and we should let him finish what he started. Moreover, this destruction of Iraq is good for me. We let corporations clean up their own pollution. We let the police in cities like Los Angeles investigate their own misconduct, so why shouldn't we let the Bush Team finish the job they started in Iraq?

Patriot Act

Terrorism is the new fear on the block, and it's working to keep America great. Fear of something unknown that could be happening anywhere at anytime is a great way to keep Americans on edge. Many Americans have yet to catch on, and we need to keep it that way if we want to stay great.

A Final Word on Fear

The history of fear is clear; the more fear leaders and governments can instill in their populace, the greater the nation is. From Rome, to Britain, and the United States, fear has made countries great.

We must be constantly vigilant and keep our fear in hand at all times. The government, corporations, and the media are an essential part in this fear creation. The citizens of this great nation must do their part.

Where there's hope, we must create fear. Where there is trust, provoke suspicion. When neighbors work together, remind them that neighbors kill and steal and want what you have. When diplomacy might work, we must threaten the enemy. Mediation is a tool of the communist, terrorist, and liberal. The only way I want to mediate with someone is through the barrel of my Colt 45. It's what makes America great. Next, I will talk about one of the greatest fears of all: *The Liberal Juggernaut.*

Chapter II

The Liberal Juggernaut

Liberals are such treacherous liars that we must constantly call them names. In this chapter, I unrelentingly state my truth about liberals. What is a liberal? A liberal is someone who wants to change everything so that no one has to work and everyone lives off government handouts. Liberals live off the hard work of the rest of us Christian conservatives.

I prove in this chapter that liberals are no good, pro-terrorist, devil worshipping, America hating, lazy scum. Therefore, every time I mention liberal in this chapter and in this book, you know that a liberal is bad, has always been bad, and will be bad in times to come and must be avoided. You must sneer when you read the word liberal, for the flag, for America.

Liberals are like a flu virus that won't go away. No matter how many branches of government we Neocons control (at least three by my count), the liberals won't give up. That is what makes them so dangerous.

This country is getting richer and richer every day, so why aren't liberals happy? Liberals, no matter how rich they are, won't be happy until communists have taken over our country. You would think that Al Franken and Michael Moore would stop yelling by now; they are, after all, rich. They are getting rich off all the gullible liberals to whom they have been lying.

The only explanation for their continued yelling is that they hate America and freedom and they love the ill-gotten money they get from lying. They don't like it when Republicans and conservatives (the people) rule. It is true that most people in America are conservative; therefore, we *should* rule everything.

Liberals today control the media, the education system, science, the government, judges, and the comic book industry (just look at those superheroes in their tights and fancy costumes being do-gooders!). With all this liberal control of our daily lives, we conservatives must fight back with our greatest tools: our patriotism, our *manly firmness,* the flag, righteousness and our skills handling the truth.

Eric Alterman writes for The Nation magazine and says that the idea of a liberal media is a "useful myth" (What Liberal Media? The Truth About Bias and the News). Hell, a liberal writing for a liberal rag is saying that it's not liberal. Well, all criminals say they're innocent, and we all know they're guilty. All liberals who say that there is not a liberal media are lying because they're liberals writing in the media thus making the media liberal. Of course, just being a liberal makes Mr. Alterman wrong.

If there are hundreds of conservative talk show hosts, thousands of conservative journalists, dozens of conservative papers, a multitude of right-wing web sites and ultra conservative writers like me saying liberals control the media, they do. Did you know that every time Michael Moore puts out a movie, the terrorist have a big party for him? That's how fiendishly clever the liberals are and how much control they have.

If I told you that a tree had four legs, thick orange fur, and a pointed snout, would you believe me? You wouldn't, would you, unless you were a knee-jerk liberal. Then why would you allow liberals to define what a conservative is for you? Well, here's news for you:

- Liberals enjoy sex and don't care about the unborn children that could be made with the wasted sperm and female eggs that aren't getting fertilized.
- Liberals hate America and would rather live under the rule of Saddam Hussein than defend our country using a gun.
- Liberals dislike freedom and the Second Amendment, and they won't defend themselves when attacked.
- Liberals would rather complain about the Iraq War than turn in their terrorist neighbor because they don't want to be called politically incorrect.
- Liberals would rather teach tolerance than kill strangers in countries far away.

So why would anyone ever believe the lies that liberals tell about America or us?

What True Patriotic Conservatives Are Up Against

Now you might wonder, dear reader, why people would vote for and support outrageously rich companies and individuals (like myself) over the interests of their own class (the poor). Well, why shouldn't average folks vote to help the wealthy? They're just supporting the winning team. Like seventy-two virgins waiting in heaven for terrorists (a claim terrorists make when recruiting suicide bombers), supporting the winning team is your ticket into the Promised Land and might land you a job cleaning out our country clubs in heaven. The under-educated poor and the insulated rich are the winning side that keeps America safe from the liberal scum that controls our nation.

Here's a short list (due to time constraints) of the liberal things to watch out for as you start each day:

- The Media
- The Government

- Democrats and some Republicans
- Entertainment (Liberaltainment)
- Education (especially teachers)
- Science (especially biology)

Start each day with a prayer, "I will not listen to the liberal media, nor be duped by the liberal government, nor the entertainment industry, nor teachers, nor scientists. I will close my mind to all thoughts that create cognitive dissonance such as thoughts that may change my mind and make me more liberal." Then you will be safe.

The Liberal Media

The only way to counteract the liberal control of the media is to reduce their presence on television and the radio to almost nothing and to make things up about them until they get embarrassed and go away. As soon as we get rid of that dangerous Bill Moyers, we can reduce the threat level to "elevated" (yellow). The liberal media is as dangerous as a bull at a quadriplegic rodeo-clown convention.

We know liberals control the media because Pat Buchanan, Ann Coulter, Bill O'Reilly, Rush Limbaugh, Michael Savage, David Horowitz, Robert Novak, George Will, and dozens of other wise journalists tell us so. All of these folks tell us that the media is liberal, and so do I. And so it is. If a right-wing reporter calls the media liberal, it is liberal. That is all the proof you need to have. It's a wonder any Republicans get elected at all the way the media is against them. News is controlled by liberal reporters, not the corporate bosses and editors of papers that could fire those reporters if they disagreed with the corporate talking points.

How we know that the media is out to get us conservatives

Where's God? If you don't mention God in every broadcast or newspaper article, you're a hell bound liberal that should be taken away and sent to China for re-education.

Where's the money? Why all this talk about *increased unemployment* for the poor folks? The richest folks are doing well under Bush. However, the liberal media doesn't report that. If people can't make do on two minimum wage jobs, they're just lazy.

Why is there all this "entertainment news"? I'm tired of seeing all these liberal folk on red carpets strutting around in fancy gowns thinking they're better than us. If the media weren't liberal, we'd see more Miss America and less *Oscars*. At least Country Music Television is patriotic enough to show

Miss America. In fact, we should have a "Miss America Channel" with 24-hour pageantry. Now that's American! While we're at it, we could have the NRA channel too. We could call it "The Shooting Channel".

The media covers liberal issues and not issues that patriots like us have concern

Intelligent Design: Whenever the liberal media talks about *Intelligent Design*, the liberal press seems to feel they need to mention "evolution". Why is that? Because they hate God!

Terry Sciavo: The poor woman was doing well living on a machine and the liberal media seemed to feel that living in a vegetative state indefinitely was the worst thing possibly. How dare the media even question what the White House thinks!

Education: What irks me is that the liberal media is always talking about "public" education. Why do you only hear the lunch menus for public schools and not private schools announced on the radio? Big deal if over 90% of all students go to public schools. That doesn't mean you should focus only on them. The liberal media just hates it when people have a choice because they support terrorism and communism and only people who admire the likes of Hitler and Saddam Hussein are against choice. Liberals hate it when people get a choice because they were the nerdy kids who were selected last in the dodge ball game.

Constitutional Rights: Who needs the Bill of Rights and who is that Habeas Corpus that everyone is talking about anyway? You would have thought that the United States had detained people indefinitely in the past. Okay, there was that whole Japanese internment during WWII, detentions of US citizens of German decent during WWI, and Haitians in Florida for being, well, Haitian and not Cuban refugees, and so forth. But that was because we needed protection. I'll explain that later because detention is a "tool of democracy".

What we need to stop are all these references to the Constitution. The founding fathers didn't have Islamic Terrorists from Iraq (because you know the terrorists were from Iraq on 9/11, right?) driving planes into their buildings leaving 57,000 victims. At least the Red Cross estimates that it *helped* 57,000 people affected by 9/11. The founding fathers didn't have to deal with car bombs, or wagon bombs or horse bombs or whatever in 1776 when the people wrote the Constitution.

You won't hear the liberal media talk about how the founding fathers were weak on terrorism and how we now have a final solution for this problem. Our great President won't listen to this talk about rights and all because he's got things to protect in the U.S. He won't let rights get in the way of the defense of free trade and profits.

Clinton Scandals: Why didn't we hear more about all the women Bill Clinton was having sex with when he was in the White House? We should have heard more, and more often, about the Monica Lewinsky affair. We would have if the media weren't so liberal.

Bush and Iraq: Can you believe some reporters had the gall to suggest Bush lied about the Iraqi threat? Those liberals!

The media is liberal because they don't talk about, at all times, what the Right finds important. Thankfully, our vast armies of watchdogs on television, radio, the press, and the internet are out there trying to stop the liberal control of the media.

How to Run a Patriotic Presidential Press Conference

The rabidly liberal media asks all sorts of nasty questions of the President about WMD and tax cuts for the rich. That is why we keep them out of *our* press conferences. Here's a handy guide to future journalist on how to ask questions of the commander and chief:

Always start questions with compliments, such as, "As the great president that you are..." or "As a popular world leader..." or "As a man of the people..." and so forth.

Only ask leading questions that give the president the answer beforehand, "As a great leader, how will you bring democracy to Iraq through elections?" or "As a great leader, how will you bring us into the 21st century with wise and sustainable alternative fuel programs?"

Ask questions of faith while avoiding asking for facts: "Do you believe Iraq will be better off in the future?" or "Do you believe Iran has a nuclear weapons program?" or "Do you believe the Cubs will win a World Series in your lifetime?"

Ask closed ended questions that the President can answer with a yes or a no.
Q: "Does Iraq pose a threat to the United States?"
A: Yes.
Q: "Is the economy improving?"
A: Yes.
Q: "Is abstinence only education working?"
A: Yes.
Q: "Are the Democrats tax and spend liberals?"
A: Yes.

Q: "Should we increase spending on social programs?"
A: No.
Q: "Should we increase spending on no-bid contracts for government work."
A: Yes.
And so on.
Don't ask follow-up questions that look for answers to unanswered questions.

Finally, *if* we Neocons happen to control *some* media, it is the natural course of things in a Darwinian economy. We like Darwin when we talk about survival of the fittest in economic terms. Billionaires just wonder what Darwin has to do with how humans arrived on the planet.

What we want to make clear is that even though Billionaires own the media and run its functions as the heads of mega media conglomerates, the press and media are liberal. We have the power to hire and fire those reporters who don't think like we do, but it's liberals that run things. We can censor programs that are not allied with what we believe (such as *The Reagans* movie on CBS that wasn't flattering Ronnie enough for us), but it's liberals that set the agenda. Liberals are pesky, and they infect America with their ideology through the media that *we* own.

Liberal Government in the U.S.

The government is the enemy. They're liberal, and thank God we have George Bush to stop them when he's right minded enough. Liberals might tell you that Bush takes too many vacations and doesn't work hard enough. However, what he's really doing by taking all that time off, physically and mentally, is slowing down the damage government can do. If he works less, the government gets less done. Thus, the country is protected from the government by means of presidential inefficiency. John McCain is sure to follow President Bush's lead.

Nonetheless, Bush and his liberal cabinet should not be confused with chickens laying golden eggs. They do many liberal things: they let immigrants in, they pay welfare mothers, they allow abortions, they let smut onto the airwaves, and they constrain free markets just to save a few thousand jobs in factories when we could be getting cheaper goods from China and Burma. The Bush White House has also refused to jail all traitorous liberals who are out to ruin America. That's why we true conservatives must be constantly vigilant.

Activist Judges are out to get us

Activist judges want to make guns illegal except for criminals and the jackbooted thugs at the Agency of Tobacco and Firearms that go around killing

A Patriot's Guide to Right-Wing Thinking

people. Tell me where it says in the Constitution that we can make laws up to stop people from owning guns, and I'll eat my hat.

Judges never thought about "cruel and unusual punishment" when the Branch Davidians were forced to listen to heavy-metal music in Waco, Texas. Then the government's jack-booted thugs in the ATF killed them. The Branch Davidians were a religious group. They were lead by David Koresh who the government accused of abusing children as an excuse to attack them in Waco, Texas. The Clintons, who don't respect freedom of religion, ran the government. Because a few ATF officers got killed, they surrounded the compound of the Davidians with tanks and killed them. Ninety Branch Davidians died along with four ATF agents.

I guess torture was okay with the liberal judges in this case because their hero Clinton was behind it. If James Dobson compared the Supreme Court with the KKK on his radio show "Focus on the Family" then they must be just like the hooded racists. However, I wonder what Dobson has against the KKK (Media Matters 3).

Activist judges want to tell us when and with whom we can marry. If gay marriage becomes legal everywhere, like judges ruled was legal in Massachusetts and California, then the next thing you know is they'll be forcing me, a red-blooded, purebred, American male, to marry some sissy boy. It's got to be stopped here! No wonder so many married people are getting divorced with all those sexy, sweaty, homo hunks of manliness tugging good intentioned American hetero men to the dark side like Batman and Robin or Luke and Darth Vader.

Now the government wants to tell people when to die. Only the President should be able to tell you when to die. However, people in Oregon and anti-lifers from the left coast want to change all that. Activist judges have sided with the "right to die" people in Oregon with their "right to die" law and the abortionist baby killers so many times that I could shoot myself. We'll stop those who hate life if we have to kill each and every one of them with our constitutionally protected guns. God bless America.

Now, you might find yourself living in a shotgun shack watching Pat Buchanan on the T.V. You might feel all smug and safe because the party of the rich, the Republicans, is in Washington protecting the profits of the Billionaires for whom you are lucky enough to work. But we're not safe! The Republican Party has been infiltrated with liberalism, and we have to stop it now! There are actually Republicans that vote for education bills and don't think we should invade Iran and Syria without thinking about it first.

These liberal Republicans have stopped the privatization of Social Security, thus they have cut into our profits. They have voted against flag burning amendments. They won't even consider amending the Constitution so a good foreign freunde like Arnie Schwartznegger can run for President.

Here's a short list of liberal Republican's:

- John McCain—Senator, Arizona. He dared to run against a Bush. He once said he'd let his daughter choose whether to keep a baby if she were pregnant. Moreover, he *never, ever* called Kerry unpatriotic during the 2004 election! He's recently toeing the line better, so perhaps we can stop hating him so much. As he runs for President, I better see him wearing his flag pin everywhere he goes, including the shower!
- Olympia Snowe—U.S. senator from Maine, a state with French speakers, and she's Greek! French and Greek, a dangerous combination!
- Robert W. Packwood—U.S. Senator from Oregon. Anyone who lets the feminazis kick him out of the Senate for making a few off color jokes about fornicating with women doesn't deserve our support. There were only ten women who accused him of sexual harassment. I don't see why he had to resign.
- George Pataki—Former Governor of New York -His last name sounds funny, he's from New York, and he signed comprehensive health care into law. That legislation provided health insurance coverage for more citizens. He's definitely a commie.
- Rudolph W. Giuliani—Former mayor of New York. He's from New York, and he is in favor of abortion. Moreover, he let Hillary Rodham Clinton (she-devil!) into the Senate by losing to her in 2000. He shall never be forgiven! Even though he is Mr. 9/11 and all, and Clinton lost to Obama, we still hate him. He thinks being gay is okay, for Chris's sake!

The Democrats are so clever that they even create liberals of Republicans. Will they never stop?

Liberaltainment

The entertainment industry is killing America. It's no wonder the French and Arabs hate us. I would hate us too if the only movies I saw in my country were by Steven Spielberg or featured liberals like Tim Robbins and Susan Sarandon. Therefore, liberals are the real cause of terrorism because the Arabs hate us for the cultural invasion from Hollywood, and Hollywood is sending its product all over the world.

The bombings of 9/11 wouldn't have happened without the *Die Hard* movies giving terrorists pointers on how to bomb big buildings and getting them to hate us for our cultural influence. If the religiously fundamental Arabs had only gotten to know the true essence of the fundamentalist leaders in this country, they would have seen how much our leadership and their leadership have in common in terms of religiosity and the need to control public thought. Then they wouldn't have attacked us.

Television is not entertainment. Television is a subversive undermining of our country by liberals who want to create lazy welfare mothers who will easily become comrades in arms during the liberals' communist revolution. On television you have your *Desperate Housewives* teaching American girls that it's okay to enjoy sex, and that must stop. The same goes for that *Sex in the City*. They did get one thing right: all those actresses are whores, so why not let them portray themselves like prostitutes. If people watched Fox Television News, they would learn the truth about the dangers of television.

Television sets a bad example for children. Not only does TV teach young girls that they can be independent, have careers (see The Mary Tyler Moore Show, Maud, Alice and Charlie's Angels) and that women can enjoy sex, but it teaches American children that being gay is okay. Some gay media watchers like James Dobson and his group *Focus on the Family* have berated *SpongeBob Square Pants* for being a tool of the gays to promote the gay agenda (Kirkpatrick). They must also hate Barney the purple dinosaur, Big Bird, and Clifford the Big Red Dog. There's also Velma from *Scooby-Doo*, Peppermint Patty of the *Peanuts*', and *Sesame Street*'s Ernie and Bert to gay up the screen. I'm sure that "Big Bird" is really just gay speak for something Bert gives Ernie between shows.

Gays, who are all liberal, have always controlled television. However, it wasn't until Billy Crystal played a fag on TV in *Soap* that they were in the television shows. Now those fags just can't help but put themselves into every television show out there. You have your *Ellen* show, *Will and Grace,* and *Batman* with his "Robin the Boy Wonder". Even your manly *NYPD Blue* had an openly gay receptionist. We should not be teaching this kind of tolerance of others. It's not Christian. If we're tolerant, we won't be afraid, and we need our fear to remain great.

Education and Teachers

Schools and Universities are way too liberal, and that's a bad thing. Just ask U.S. Rep. Jack Kingston, a Savannah Republican, who in October 2003 introduced a bill that clearly stated that there is not a diversity of opinion at the universities and they are promoting liberalism. Senate Republicans held a hearing on the university issue of liberal teaching; liberal professors must be recruiting, just like gays. It must be a problem in the United States. If Congress holds a hearing on something such as Elian Gonzalez or flag burning, it's a problem.

None other than David Horowitz, once liberal shill now turned conservative hero, says the universities are teaching kids to be liberal. As if teachers were somehow experts in a field because they have a PhD. Professors think twenty years of researching a field gives them the right to teach students facts. It doesn't Mr. PhD. Man! Horowitz saw the light in the seventies and came over to the side God intended, the far-right side.

David Horowitz runs the online magazine Frontpage.com. He also heads the war against professor malfeasance. Professor malfeasance is when professors think they can give bad grades on a test when the student clearly just had a different political viewpoint. He also started *Students for Academic Freedom*, a center for sending in complaints about teachers' left-wing bias.

The point is, your political or spiritual view of reality shouldn't get you bad grades if you disagree with the standard, commonly accepted, and verified scientific theory. Therefore, when the professor wants to teach you about the earth's rotation around the sun, tell him he's wrong because God created man as the center of the universe.

When a teacher tells you about sexual reproduction, tell her that Jesus was born of a virgin. When those professors want to teach about evolution, tell them God created the earth. The big bang? No, God created the earth. Fossils? They couldn't be more than five thousand to six thousand years old because, God created the earth. You must refuse to be taught because it contradicts your views as a Christian and American.

Here's how this could work to your benefit

- If you have a Chemistry 101 quiz and the sneaky professor asks you about the atomic weight of something tricky, say oxygen, just say "1". When he marks it wrong, tell him he is oppressing your beliefs as a Taoist, and that in the Taoist faith, everything is one.
- On that physics midterm, if you can't remember Kepler's laws of period and rate, just tell them as a Buddhist, you know time is an illusion, and thus there is no answer to that question.
- When studying for health science, and they ask you for a way to prevent AIDS and you can't remember (and don't they know only sinners and fags get AIDS), tell them you're a Wiccan (witch) and a sage smudge (burning of sage in your house) will cure all ailments.
- What's gravity? God's way of getting Adam that apple.
- Why is the sky blue? Zeus rides in his chariot across the sky every day. And don't oppress me when I tell the class.

- Why is there poverty? My beliefs tell me there is no poverty and you're oppressing me.
- How was the earth formed? You can bring out the old Sumerian Enuma Elish myth for the answer to that question.

Do you see how brilliant Horowitz and his followers are? If all beliefs are equal, you never have to learn what they teach in school and your soul will be saved. Whatever you believe *is* the truth, not what they teach. Remember, the universities are recruiting liberals by educating people, so keep your kids out. Uneducated masses, and the have-mores, are our base.

Teachers are recruiting liberals by making them think and question the great leaders of this country (Bush and his team). Questioning anything a leader ever does, leads to doubt, and doubt leads to seeking answers, and answer seeking can lead to reading from the Bible, the Torah, the Tao Te Ching, Hindu texts and the Koran. Reading the Koran leads to terrorism, so don't go down that slippery slope. Remember, learning is the gateway to terrorism. If your teacher doesn't toe the party line, turn him (or God forbid her) into TIPS (see chapter 1).

Dr. Teresa Whitehurst, a liberal if I ever read one, wrote an article called "Careful Not to Get Too Much Education...Or You Could Turn Liberal" (Whitehurst). See? Even liberals admit it! She tells us that just like all the gays, the liberals are recruiting in our schools and we better stop it. Dr. Teresa calls this liberal education a "devil's snare" and freely admits that she, as a liberal, is trying to ensnare her students. Too much exposure to science, philosophy, literature and diversity, can lead to such widespread tendencies. So please dear folks, keep your kids away from college and home school them.

People in school are questioning what happens in this great country far too much these days. Whom can we blame? The teachers. If you learned anything in chapter one, "Be Afraid; Be Very Afraid", you learned that tolerance just isn't good for our country. Education leads to a reduction of fear of others; it weakens us, and it must be stopped. If it's true that the more schooling you have, the more liberal you are, then it's clear that they are getting liberal ideas from the liberal teachers.

Science (especially biology)

Scientists have lots of education in universities, and unless they have repented and work for the President denouncing global warming, they are all liberal. Those good scientists working with the President didn't get too educated, so they are qualified to work for the White House.

The Liberal Juggernaut

Scientists study things that people should learn about in church: sex, life and death, space, time and gravity, magnetism, water, global warming (which doesn't exist because it's not in the bible!), medicine, genes, stem cells, and all sorts of other things. Don't waste your life with science. Science is liberal and wants to change everything and take away your freedom.

Let's look at medicine. It's dangerous and liberal. Doctors in Oregon say it's okay to die if you live in agony and pain, and won't recover and you have given your consent with two witnesses to die after being checked out for sanity. Jesus suffered for you; shouldn't you suffer in agony a little here on earth to show you really care?

Liberals don't care about life; they care about quality of life. We conservatives don't really care about how people suffer here and now because your reward is in heaven. Only God can pull the plug on the artificial lung, kidney or liver machine that is keeping you alive. Conservatives want you to live and die in a natural way, and it's not natural to pull the plug on man made machines that keep you alive.

God created all life on earth. Stem cells are from the same sacred life that God created, but are the devil's creation because scientists work with them. Most doctors, by the fact that they are scientists, are liberal. Except when helping out Reagan or saving Dick Cheney from a heart attack, they are doing evil things. Now these doctors want to take cells from frozen embryos that are going to be thrown away and use them for living humans to cure diseases. God created the trash can so these cells could be thrown away. Life is sacred, and using stems cells to save life is just wrong.

I could go on, but let's talk about this Global Warming hoax. First off, what good is the environment if we can't exploit it for human expansion and use? Besides, things aren't that bad anyway. How dare scientists use scare tactics to make us believe what they want and scare us into taking action. Scientist should be ashamed using the global warming scare to control American public opinion. What they claim is ridiculous.

Michael Crichton, the eminent writer of the groundbreaking Jurassic Park science series and science reader, thinks global warming is a bunch of cow pies (Crichton). As he writes about the dangers of using embryos in Jurassic Park, he also speaks about the dangers of the global warming hoax.

Mr. Crichton realizes humans don't create global warming, but that aliens from other planets cause it. He even tells us in his lecture, *Aliens Cause Global Warming* on January 17, 2003 (ibid), "I am going to argue that extraterrestrials lie behind global warming." So relax and keep using your aerosol spray.

Another person who writes about the global warming hoax is James K. Glassman. Writing for <u>Capitalist Magazine</u>, a magazine that has no investment in the global warming debate and is completely unbiased, Mr. Glassman tells us that Republican Senators are against global warming (Glassman). If Republican Senators don't believe in global warming, then we shouldn't either. That makes sense to me. Since cutting back on greenhouse gases would only mean fewer millions for me, members of Congress, Mr. Crichton, and Mr. Glassman, why should we care if the air is polluted?

I don't live in a superfund clean up site, a place so contaminated special government funds are spent to clean it up. If you do live in one of these sites, whose fault is that? Maybe things are getting warmer, but it's just aliens doing it.

Conclusion: We must stop the liberal destruction of our way of life

Liberals control everything and want to destroy our way of life by teaching tolerance and decreasing the fear by promoting a gay, Jewish, lazy, race-filled, scientific, God-hating, devil-worshiping agenda. Although Republicans and Conservatives only represent and work for the wealthiest 1% of society, you should support us because we are better than liberals. What's good for the richest 1% is good for the country as a whole even if *you* are worse off. Remember:

- The mightiest counterpart to the Conservative is represented by the Liberal.
- Existence impels the Liberal to lie, and to lie perpetually, just as it compels the inhabitants of northern lands to wear warm clothing.
- Was there any form of filth or shamelessness, particularly in cultural life, without at least one Liberal involved in it? If you cut even cautiously into such an abscess, you found—like a maggot in a rotting body often dazzled by the sudden light—a little Liberal.
- No one need be surprised if among our people the personification of the devil as the symbol of all evil assumes the living shape of the Liberal.
- The Liberal doctrine of Marxism rejects the aristocratic principle of Nature and replaces the eternal privilege of power and strength with the mass of numbers and their dead weight. Thus, it denies personal worth, contests the significance of folk and race, and thereby withdraws from mankind premise for its existence and culture. As a foundation of the universe, it would lead to the end of any order intellectually conceivable to man. . . If, with the help of his Marxist creed, the Liberal is victorious over the peoples of the world, his crown will be the funeral wreath of mankind and this planet will—as it once did for millions of years—move through the ether devoid of men.

The Liberal Juggernaut

- Hence today I believe that I am acting in accordance with the will if the Almighty Creator: *by resisting the* Liberal, *I am fighting for the work of the Lord.*
- There can be no making pacts with the Liberal, but only the hard: either—or.
- For a racially pure people who are conscious of its blood can never be enslaved by the Liberal. In this world he will forever be master over bastards alone.

By the way, this last section was taken from that brilliant read, <u>Mein Kampf</u>, written by that Hitler fellow. The word Jew was taken out, and Liberal was put in its place. It fits just as well and is true for us today as it was for the Nazis back then. It is clear from these words that liberals are the enemy, and we must find whatever final solution we can for the liberals.

Chapter III

Why You're Poor, and Why it's Your Fault

There are poor people and there are rich people in America. We all have our place, and it's nice to see that the American people are willing to stay in theirs. It's survival of the fittest that creates the natural balance between the rich and the poor in America, and we will do everything we can to make sure this balance is maintained.

With the help of Ayn Rand, Milton and Thomas Friedman, Adam Smith, and other experts on economics, I explain "Why You're Poor and Why it's Your Fault." Experts will help me explain that being less than rich is your fault, there really aren't poor people in America, and that the government is to blame if you are poor.

Billionaires promote personal responsibility. This includes consumer spending. I know that if you consumed more, you wouldn't be poor. I also know that Congress passes tax laws that benefit the wealthy, and they pass cuts to education and health care funding while they raise costs at universities and hospitals. It's your fault we cut social spending. Let's not forget that while Congress keeps giving themselves raises (cost of living adjustments), the minimum wage has gone up once since 1997. If Congress passes more wage increases, I might have to move to Mexico to avoid the liberal takeover of our great nation.

In the end, it's your fault that you have no money and the minimum wage is low. A COLA (cost-of-living adjustment) increase for Congressional pay was passed in 1987. Congress automatically gets a pay raise every year unless they take action to cancel it. Can you imagine Congress taking action on anything, especially to cut their own pay raises? Vice President Cheney and Supreme Court justices will see increases in their paychecks as Congress does.

Why haven't you gotten your own COLA through Congress? It's not our fault your real wages, wages compared to inflation, are going down. Don't come begging to us when you want a pay raise. The free market sets wages, and it's when the government interferes with the market rate of wages that we're vulnerable to terrorism.

The problem with the Poor

Dr. Walter E. Williams, a black man and economist, agrees. He says, "If you're a poor adult in America, for the most part, it's all your fault. That's true, at least today, whether you're black, white, brown or polka dot." He adds,

> Let's look at poverty in female-headed households. Divorce and death of the father might explain a small part of why there're so many female-headed households. But the bulk of it is explained by people having children and not getting married in the first place. For the most part, female-headed households are the result of short-sighted, self-destructive behavior of one or two people.
>
> According to an NPR/Kaiser/Kennedy School Poll, the leading cause of poverty identified by both the poor (75 percent) and non-poor (65 percent) was drug abuse. Again, it's not like you're walking down the street and you're struck with drug addiction; to use drugs is a conscious decision. Drug-users tend not to be very productive. They drop out of school, abandon their families, have scrapes with the law and don't hold down jobs. Would anybody be surprised that poverty is one result of drug usage? (Williams)

What Dr. Williams is saying is that it's your fault if you're poor because you're probably a slutty single mother or a drug addict. The rich like me are able to buy access and have laws passed to make us richer by taking money from you. Why don't you buy influence from your own Congressman?

Even with such incontrovertible proof as presented by Dr. Williams, there still seems to be some liberals who think marriage is not the answer. Take Diana Spatz, please. She writes as if she knows something warm-blooded American men don't:

> Clearly, marriage is not a solution for mothers who face domestic violence, as I once did.
>
> Yet, at the same time, Mr. Bush's proposed budget for 2005 slashes child-care funding for 300,000 low-income kids. Given the high unemployment rate, his proposal is likely to force states to create massive "workfare" programs to meet increased work participation rates at a cost of $11 billion to the states. However, my deepest concern with the proposal is that it ignores hard truths: For many low-income parents in my state, neither marriage nor work is enough to get their families off welfare, let alone out of poverty.
>
> In 2003, more than 130,000 parents in California reached their five-year lifetime limit on welfare, and were cut off public assistance for the rest of their lives - even though up to 92 percent of them were working and playing by the rules. (Spatz)

Why You're Poor, and Why it's Your Fault

As far as I know, Spatz is not a Republican, a police officer, a businessman, nor a corporate leader, so what does she know about domestic violence? As if stating a few facts would puncture the balloon of Bush's wisdom. Clearly, if women are being hit, it's their fault. With the lip on Ms. Spatz, I can tell you whose fault that was. She was probably mouthing off during the Super Bowl. Football is just too important to let a marriage get in way.

Not only are you to blame for being poor, you're not really poor after all. According to Robert E. Rector and Kirk Johnson, PhD., the poor in America really aren't poor (Rector). They have stats to prove it, and those stats come from the government, who we know always gets their facts right. Rector and Johnson tell us that of the 35 million people in "poverty" in the United States:

- 46% of the "poor" own their own home.
- 66% of the "poor" have air conditioning. Heck, I, Tex, have air conditioning, so they must be living high on the hog.
- Almost 75% of the "poor" own a car, and 30% of them own two cars. As Reagan once said, "Welfare mothers drive Cadillacs." He was right!
- 75% of these households own a color television. When are the poor going to watch TV between their two jobs?
- 62% have cable or satellite TV reception. What Mr. Rector and Johnson fail to point out is that most of these poor folks steal the cable access.
- The "poor" even own microwaves, 73%; stereos, more than 50%; and a third have an automatic dishwasher.

When you add up all the above percents, you have 46% (homeowners) +66% (air conditioning) +75% (Cars) +75% (Color TVs) +73% (microwaves) +50% (dishwasher). That's way over 100%. In fact, it tells us that 385 percent of these families really aren't poor because they own these luxury items.

As you now know, there are no more poor people in the United States. When the government says there are 35 million poor households in this country, that's just not true. It's their fault *if* they are poor. The poor should have a big _P_ tattooed on their forehead so the rest of us know to avoid them on the street. We should get a warning when the poor come our way.

There's more from Rector and Johnson to know. They say that 58% of these "poor" households didn't experience any hardship at all. Therefore, only 20.3 million Americas really had any hardship in 2005. Big deal! That's less than two-thirds the population of California. They conclude with the good news. Although there are more poor in America, supposedly, the poor are better off than they were in the past. Thanks to credit cards, they can afford televisions, heating (a luxury if I ever heard of one) and food. So, keep it up you poor, you're doing great.

Bad Behavior: Eleven Real Reasons You're Poor

According to the 1990 U.S. Census Bureau and the Institute for Policy Innovation, the causes of poverty are behavioral, economical, and medical. Behavioral decisions were found as the leading cause of poverty with 64% of the respondents, 21% for economic conditions and 15% said they were poor due to illness or disability. There you are. If the poor behaved better, they wouldn't be poor.

Liberals think social factors like childhood and spousal abuse, parental drug addiction, growing up poor, mental illness, bad schools, lack of education or job skills, racial, sexual, and age discrimination, drug riddled neighborhoods, gun violence, low wages, unemployment, jobs moving overseas, rising health care costs, racial redlining and what not have something to do with poverty. They're wrong. It's just that the poor are bad apples that make bad decisions.

- When you get knocked up without marrying the dad, you could become poor.
- If you marry the women you got pregnant, you might become poor. Men would be better off (richer) if they just didn't show up anymore after that. Just let the women deal with it. It's their fault they got pregnant anyway.
- Not using birth control can lead to pregnancy and poverty. Although using birth control is a sin and you'll go to hell if you use it, it does prevent pregnancy. No one taught you about birth control? What a shame.
- When you chose to be born and stay in a poor family, you'll be poor. Poor families stay poor, so why did you choose to start there? Haven't you heard about the book <u>The Secret</u>? Just visualize yourself out of poverty if you're poor.
- When you choose to go to public schools instead of paying the paltry $10,000 a year for the cheapest private school, you'll be poor.
- If you stay in a poor neighborhood when there are better ones to live in for twice the rent, you'll be poor.
- If people would accept Jesus into their heart, they would accept their fate and stop calling themselves poor. That, in turn, would reduce the official number of poor in the United States.
- If you studied medicine, you wouldn't be poor; you wouldn't have to pay expensive doctors' bills or hospital costs.
- If you would stop being Black or Latino, you might not be poor. Why do people insist on belonging to a racial minority that is known for being poor?

- Being in a gang can keep you poor. If you would only take a few beatings now and again, the gang members might stop recruiting you.
- If you voted Republican, you wouldn't be poor or you wouldn't care. Why do you think the rich are rich? They vote Republican. Voting Republican makes you better off.

The Hellfare State Keeps You Poor

Another cause of poverty in the United States is the welfare state. William W. Beach came up with a study in 2005 called *The 2005 Index of Dependency*. It can be found on the unbiased Heritage Foundation website (Beach 2). The basic idea of this study is that the government has made us dependent on them and that is why we are getting poorer and losing our "spirit of independence and self-improvement (ibid)."

In the past, there were so few government programs. Churches and charities took care of the people, and everything was fine. Look at the Great Depression. The charities and individuals were doing fine until Comrade Roosevelt got elected in 1932 and came up with his New Deal and ruined everything by creating jobs and giving people a sense of self-worth.

Beach says housing assistance, health care, welfare, retirement care, education, and rural and agricultural services make people dependent on the government. He has this chart called the "Index of Dependency Value" (ibid) that he uses to prove more people are dependent on the government, and because of that, it's the government's fault people are poor. It works for me. Remember, the reason people go on public assistance has nothing to do with social factors or economic downturns. It's their fault and they should stop sucking on the teet of Miss America.

Reducing government help to the poor is a win-win situation. In the past, people were so much better off when they relied on the church and the Elks Club instead of the government that is supposedly "by the people, for the people". It's not the government's job to take care of people, and they don't do it very well. Therefore, we rich folk get to donate to charities to fill the need gap. We get our tax cuts for donating to the arts and the poor, we enhance our corporate image, and the deserving poor get some help.

Let's first look at housing assistance. This government assistance program keeps people poor. We know there is a level playing field in the housing markets. However, if you were to quote Jimmy Carter's communist aid organization Habitat for Humanity and their website, you would think there was a housing problem.

A Patriot's Guide to Right-Wing Thinking

> In fact, 5.1 million American families have "worst-case" housing needs, forced to pay more than half their income for housing, endure overcrowded conditions and/or live in houses with severe physical deficiencies. While the number of families in poverty is growing, the number of affordable rental units is shrinking, and most families who qualify for government housing assistance aren't receiving any aid (Habitat for Humanity).

If families want to stop paying half their rent for housing, why don't they just earn more money? These commies from Habitat for Humanity ignore the first rule of economics: the free market knows best, and people need to adjust to the market. No correction is necessary. Profit is benign, profit is good, the hardworking owners of run-down expensive apartments are only looking for a hard-earned dollar, and the renters are just lazy riff-raff.

For example, there are janitors in Silicon Valley that earn $17,000 dollars a year (2006 dollars) from generous corporations like Sun Microsystems, Apple and Oracle, but people are complaining. Take out 20% out for taxes, and that leaves them with huge amount of $13,600 a year. I found a one-bedroom apartment near Silicon Valley for $850.00 a month in the San Jose Mercury News in 2006, so let's look at the math. Assuming no kids or dependants, 850 x 12= $10,200 for rent. That leaves $3,200 for the rest of the expenses. Janitors can buy a yearly bus pass to get to work up front, that's $674.00 a year leaving a total of $2576.00, a luxurious $50.00 a week for food, clothes, furniture, gas, electricity, upkeep, and other expenses.

A minimum cost of $50.00 a month for gas and electricity (which means you're at work half the time with no light or gas usage) would leave $37.50 a week. That doesn't include health insurance, but I would think most janitors get free health insurance. This leaves room for sick days, because you know these janitors have good benefits and paid sick days. $37.50 a week? That's not so bad. I once only had $37.50 for booze on a plane trip in first class, and I did very well thank you.

Being a janitor at a high tech company is the first step to becoming a software engineer that earns $120,000 a year. All food stamps and housing assistance would do is make these janitors dependent on the government and keep them from their future in computer programming. Housing assistance for janitors and millions of other low-wage workers in urban America would just create the kind of dependency on the government we want to avoid. We wouldn't want the people to think the government might help them. That might get them to start voting and actual asking for redress of inequities, and that would hurt us. Let's not keep poor people dependent by helping them. Isn't housing assistance best left to the churches and shelters anyway?

Undue Burden: Health Care

I for one am sick and tired of people getting sick when they can't afford to do so. The government pays more and more money to support entitlements like Medicare and Medicaid every year and the ungrateful masses continue to get sick. Now I don't want to hear about universal health care; that's treasonous talk. Health care goes to those who deserve it the most.

The Bush government, and we can include lots of Democrats here, do their best to de-fund public health care. If more than half a million bankruptcies in 2002 were due to medical bills, that's just the cost of doing business. Thankfully, most Americans are rightfully afraid of terrorism that might ensue due to universal health care. Therefore, the market rules the prices of healthcare, and America stays strong.

Liberals in the United States government say that forty-eight million Americans are out there without health care. Big deal, that's less than 15% of the United States. The rest of us are doing fine. Why should we let a minority lead us into a ruinous single payer health care plan? They can use "single prayer" health care if they need help.

If you think people being uninsured is bad, think about the belabored HMOs and the pharmaceutical companies that are under attack by liberal do-gooders. That doesn't even count the poor insurance companies that would be hurt by national health care. According to CBS MarketWatch (Gerencher), 528 HMOs in California found that profits increased 52% during the first nine months of 2004 on the strength of higher prices for services. Like all good free market enterprises, health care charges what the market dictates. It's easy to increase premiums on a captive audience that has to pay to stay alive.

A Weiss Ratings study of financial statements filed with state insurance departments found that health maintenance organizations (HMOs) earned $6.7 billion in the first nine months of 2003, up from $4.4 billion in 2002 (ibid). Liberals, who hate profit, want to tell us that these health care companies are making too much money. If they had their way, no one would get health care in the United States. All the companies would have to shut down if we limited their profit and there would be no one left to help the sick that *can* afford health care.

If Congress supported national health care, there would be an uproar from the 952 health industry lobbyists in Washington and Congress just couldn't handle that (Public Citizen's Watch). There are also those twenty-one plus HMO and pharma donors to Bush's presidential campaign that gave $100,000 to $200,000 contributions each, not to mention the countless lobbyists working governors and state legislators that would be hurt if we had a national health care plan (Public Citizen, Congress Watch).

Congress couldn't ignore the $141,000,000 drug companies spent in support of the prescription drug bill (ibid). That bill prevented socialists from reducing medicine costs and passed the costs on to the American people through increased government spending. The compassionate United States Congress can't see it in their hearts to upset the poor downtrodden lobbyist. We need to stop health care plans that help Americans at the expense of the health care industry. Damn those liberals who support terrorism by trying to reduce drug costs.

National health care would bankrupt the country and we can't really afford it while we're sending bombs overseas. You've got to prioritize. National health care is bad, communist, and Canadian! If you deserved health care, you'd have it.

According to the White House website, Medicaid and Medicare cost $538 billion in 2006 alone (WhiteHouse.gov, Department of Health and Human Services). That money could pay for an extra Iraq war we could have every year. Why are we helping people with health care when there are wars to fight? We need to cut, cut, cut or otherwise, we would have to end the Star Wars missile defense funding. If you cut out the Star Wars program, the terrorists will be using outer space to deliver their WMDs to the United States. That terrorism would be all due to some selfish Americans who think they need health care.

Liberals say we passed the prescription drug bill to protect drug companies' big profits. There they go again, lying to the vulnerable taxpayers. We did it to protect America from terrorist Canadian drug companies. So what if drug companies made big profits on drugs. According to Forbes Magazine, pharmaceuticals were the fifth most profitable industry in 2005 (CBS Moneyline). The top nineteen companies made a total of $288,148,000,000. That's almost $300 billion dollars. They make money because free enterprise allows them to stay in business.

If you can't afford your asthma or pain medication, it's because what's really important is that the top drug companies made billions in profits in 2005. More profit means more money for stockholders. Since we're an "ownership society", as President Bush says, we *all* do better when drug companies do better.

The drug industry, along with its Congress, says that the high costs of drugs are due to the cost of research and development (R&D) of these medicines. They need profits to do research. Sure, the government gives millions of dollars to drug companies for R&D. In addition, some of the costs of research are tax write-offs (up to 34%), cutting the real cost of R&D significantly (Public Citizen's Watch). If we didn't give them this tax incentive, our medicine companies would lose out to the Germans and we'd have to take drugs from old Europe.

Drug companies spend two-and-a-half times more on marketing than research, but marketing leads to profits and more drugs. The profit they make allows more research and thus helps the pharmaceuticals stay in business. If they didn't keep promoting and creating needs for drugs, they wouldn't be able to do the research to produce the drugs for which they are creating a need.

Drug prices are set to benefit society. Supply and demand is the mechanism that set determines the prices to protect our freedoms in America. Viagra costs over $10 a pill because erections are in high demand. That is also why heart medication, obesity-reducing medication, AIDS medication, among others, cost so much. People have to survive AIDS and Cancer, and anyone who's ever watched celebrities on TV wants to be skinnier. The free market is the best way to dispense health care. As I said, Medicare and Medicaid make people dependent and lazy and cause all the healthcare problems. Can't people just go to charity hospitals if they need medical care?

Charity Hospitals fill in the gap where regular health insurance doesn't. The hospitals also know how to get money from patients by garnishing payments from people's low wages. So again, get sick at your own risk. At least we have charity hospitals that will help and keep lazy welfare cheats in line.

Because of our status at keeping America great, rich Republican boosters get extra special health care. Tennessee came up with a great way to support the rich and get the free market more involved in healthcare. The government decided that in Tennessee under TennCare that rich folks can pay a premium to be put to the head of the line at Tennessee hospitals (Herbert).

TennCare takes the decision of who to treat out of the hands of doctors, liberal humanistic scientists that they are, and into the hands of bureaucrats. Doctors would go around treating all the sick if they could. We can't afford that. Bureaucrats for the health insurance industry and government will save money by only treating those that pay extra. This is why the United States has the best health care in the world. We know who to treat and how to treat them.

The Cadillac Crimes of Welfare Mothers

Why do we support a corrupt welfare system that is so easy to abuse and that excessively benefits the poor? If a lazy liberal like Barbara Ehrenreich, who is bent on destroying the American family, can make due on low wages in her book <u>Nickeled and Dimed</u> (Ehrenreich), anybody can. She proves, by surviving with low wage jobs, that people don't really need public assistance.

The Personal Responsibility and Work Opportunity Reconciliation Act of 1996, commonly known as "welfare reform", made everything better and welfare to work is the greatest idea ever to improve welfare. If we're going to give welfare, let's make sure there is a time limit and that the poor have to go to work eventually. We know there are so many good jobs out there, so people should work.

Why are the welfare programs being abused? Welfare does not benefit everyone, so we know it's not good for anyone. Why should we pay for something that doesn't benefit us? Here are some of the new rules people on welfare have to follow:

- There is a sixty-month lifetime limit on receiving welfare.
- There is an Earned Income Tax Credit (EITC) for single welfare mothers to get tax cuts because they have dependent children. At least it goes to *real* families, one man and one woman with lots of kids, as well as single-parent households.
- The law replaces open-ended AFDC payments (Aid to Families with Dependent Children) with TANF (Temporary Aid to Needy Families) payments so that if mommy or daddy doesn't work, we won't give them food stamps. Cutting off food to children is a great way to get parents to work.
- Twenty-four month continuous TANF payments without work can lead to termination of benefits.
- Each state can dictate the length of payments. Therefore, California can stick with the sixty-month limit while South Dakota, a state that just eliminated abortion, can have a twenty-four month lifetime limit for welfare. That's how compassionate conservatism works.

Another thing I like about *Welfare to Work* is the $8,500 dollar tax credit that our corporations have received, starting in 2004, for each TANF recipient hired (U.S. Department of Labor). Not only was the money being diverted away from welfare and into Billionaires' tax cuts, our corporations get a bigger tax cut when we hire these newly expelled welfare recipients. This increases employment, keeps wages low, and keeps America safe.

Most of the single welfare mothers in America aren't married, and there is a special section in hell for unwed mothers. Why don't these women protect their families by being married? According to the National Organization of Women, 60% of the women receiving TANF are abused at home. What are a few beatings, rapes, bruises, and life threatening situations with husbands when it comes to having a nuclear family that God had in mind? Single welfare mothers are sinning twice when they first take welfare and then leave husbands or don't marry the fathers of their children. If they just put up with a little abuse, they would be better off.

William Beach is clear that if the government gets involved in helping these women and other poor people, the women would be dependent on the government just like the drugs to which they're all addicted. These women should be dependent on a man or on the charity of Christian organizations that were so prevalent before World War II. As we know, and Mr. Beach makes clear, people weren't poor or destitute before World War II, and because we know that is true, it must be because there was less government help and more Christian charities and marriages back in the good old 1930s and 40s.

When people take welfare, they're stealing from me. White people end up paying for programs for lazy people who won't get up off their asses. Sure, 40% of single mothers pay half their earnings for childcare and another 25% spend 40-50% of their income for childcare (United States Department of Health and Human Services Administration for Children and Families), but this is the land of opportunity. That means 65% of the TANF recipients have to pay 40-50% of their wages to childcare once they are forced back to work under *Welfare to Work* laws.

If the rich can afford childcare and work less than these welfare families, why can't the poor afford childcare? We cut that welfare budget, and that is good for all Americans. Why do liberals insist on whining about childcare? We believe in families and that is why we're cutting welfare.

Charles Murray's book, <u>Losing Ground</u>, makes a great case for getting rid of welfare. He uses lots of graphs and charts to prove what he says is right. He tells us that if you created incentives, incentives like keeping children hungry and malnourished, and then people go back to work. Why should Americans pay a few dollars in taxes to keep people from being hungry? The liberal New York Times did not like <u>Losing Ground</u>, so that is good enough reason to support the book and author.

Murray tells us that because of government programs like Medicaid, SSI, food stamps, subsidized housing and other crimes against Billionaires and the have-mores, the poor are losing the incentive to work. In the past, Murray says, white people were feeling so guilty that black people were poor that they felt they needed to help blacks with government programs. Mr. Murray tells us there is no reason to feel guilty for defending what is rightfully ours.

Being guilty and helping the poor is not very Christian. Christ would have wanted us to keep our billions so we could take care of our families, not the undeserving masses. "Teach a man to fish" is what Jesus would have wanted, and if the poor man has no money for an education to learn how to fish, he can gratefully clean our floors. The poor should be dependent on the rich, not the government. Murray states that blacks got lazy because we were giving them welfare and they had no incentive to be independent.

Some people complain that we rich folks create poverty by sending jobs overseas, keeping the minimum wage low, making health care costly, not providing childcare, not equipping inner city schools, and then blaming the welfare recipients. But why should we be guilty if someone can't make it? Mr. Murray justifies our wealth on the grounds that it's the government's fault that people are poor. That's all the proof I need.

If we can cut off the government tap of welfare, those living wage jobs with health care and childcare that don't exist now will miraculously appear like loaves and fishes. You don't need an education, a computer, a typewriter, or any way to create a resume'. There are lots of low wage jobs available, and they give all the benefits the poor need to retain their lifestyle.

We would like to thank Congress and President Clinton for welfare reform. The best thing about welfare reform and time limits is that they create a larger pool of surplus workers, increasing competition between workers for low wage jobs. The more workers compete, the more productive they become without us having to give them a raise.

Social Security and Elderly Greed

So far, we've learned that if you're poor it's your fault, the poor aren't really poor in the United States, and that government programs that help out citizens just create a dependence on the government. This is all true and why we also need to get rid of Social Security.

Social Security is a plan that helps retired Americans, the disabled, and people who have lost primary care givers. It was a bad idea from the start to help these people, and it just shows the greed of the elderly who refuse to go quietly. In 1935, Comrade Roosevelt decided that old folks couldn't fend for themselves, so he took money from the public to give the elderly money for living. I don't understand this need to be comfortable that old folks have.

Social Security was part of the New Deal. It was Roosevelt's plan to stick it to the rich guy. Once again, the rich are footing the bill so some lazy, in this case retired, people can stay in the homes they have lived in their whole lives. The homes of the retired in the inner cities need to be gentrified to improve the economy. Selfish retired people shouldn't get in the way of progress, and welfare is part of the problem. The elderly should be forced to go back to work so they remain contributing members of our society.

In 2005, President Bush talked frequently about the problem of Social Security. As when he made his case for WMDs in Iraq, he should have been able to convince the American people that there was a problem with Social Security. People are better off if they can give their money away to corporations to invest for them. As we all know, investing in companies such as Enron, Global Crossing, Halliburton, and internet corporations is safe. The stock market is scrupulous. Look at chapter V and you too will agree how honest corporations are and how they just want to help people.

What we know is that in the future sometime, anywhere between twenty and fifty years, the program won't be able to pay out all its obligations. Therefore, we should get rid of Social Security now. The military didn't have trouble paying its $447 billion in costs in 2004. Why can't Social Security fend for itself?

The AARP (American Association of Retired People) uses their website to create fear in order to keep money out of the hands of the suffering people on Wall Street. They want all people to live a risk free life after retirement with cost of living adjustments for its members. It just promotes the myth that retired people are getting old and can't work. They also want disability and survivor benefits to protect workers and their families. If workers decide to get injured, why should we pay for it? It's not our fault.

What makes AARP so dangerous is that its membership votes in large numbers and pays attention to elections. We must stop the selfish behavior of all these old folks who think they are owed something. They elderly only defended the country during WWII, Korea, and Vietnam wars, taught our children, cleaned our streets, were police officers and firemen, and built houses we live in. They don't deserve the money they put in to the system. Not until we get our hands on it.

Education is the Great Leveler

Another reason you're poor is that you don't understand how to educate yourself. The United States is the smartest country in the world and that's because we have the smartest schools. Education gives everyone the opportunity to advance in our society. It certainly helped President Bush.

If you're born rich, you have already proven yourself better than the lesser classes. Like our kids, you deserve the best schools. In fact, being from a wealthy family should be the only qualification our children need to get into the university of our choice. For the rest of you, education can help you advance. There are several easy steps for you to get into the university of your choice. Remember, it's up to you. The government is not here to bail you out.

First, make sure you're not born, nor live in, an inner city. They are notorious for having bad schools, like East Saint Louis, Brooklyn, and South Chicago among others. Those kids rarely go to college; in fact, only about 250 in 10,000 will graduate from college from these areas. That's 2.5% of those students (Kozol). But remember, it's your fault if you are in an inner city, so help is not on the way.

In addition, make sure you live in a two-parent household and you can afford a tutor or have one of the parents stay at home to help educate you. Make sure your parents can afford private school, or you live in a state that pays teachers higher wages. Private schools are best, but parts of Minnesota, Massachusetts and areas of Michigan have good public schools.

You could become a great athlete in football, hockey, baseball, basketball, tennis, or golf to get into college. If you're really good, you won't have to study at all when you get to college. Rich folk like me will pay hundreds of dollars to see you play with balls.

According to liberal researcher, Jonathan Kozol, the worst schools in America fail over half the student population. Many of these schools have leaky roofs, and there are not enough books for students to take home to do homework. The class sizes are up to fifty, so many of the teachers quit before the end of the year. This allows the school districts to weed out not only the bad teachers, but also the bad students.

You could "throw money at the problem", but that would just encourage potential low-wage workers (PLOWS) to stay in class and use public tax dollars better spent on wealthy children. Mr. Kozol thinks children need better buildings that actually have sufficient air and heat but he doesn't understand the reality of life in America. Good students are already in the better schools, and resources shouldn't be wasted on the bad students. If they were really good students, they wouldn't have been born poor and would be able to get into the better schools.

Here's the other thing proponents of education spending forget. You get what you pay for. Richer families pay more in property taxes for schools in their areas. Therefore, schools get more money in rich districts. This is as it should be. Rich kids are used to living better and it would be a shock to have to go to a school that didn't emulate their life style. Poor kids are used to living low, so if schools in East St. Louis are closed because of sewage overflows and toxic fumes in the city, these students will get over it.

Resources, such as lab equipment in impoverished schools, are not needed. These kids don't understand science, so why waste the money? The only science these poor kids know is how to make meth because that is what the poor learn at home. Liberals should shut up if they think that if poor kids can learn how to make meth, they can learn how to do beneficial chemistry, such as making Viagra.

These poor kids don't need recreation facilities, gyms, books, air conditioning, heating in the winter, or other facilities. The kids that are good at basketball will be drafted into the better high schools so white folks can have pride when their kids' schools win state championships. The kids at the poor schools won't need gyms because they aren't good at sports. Sports, like school, should only be for those kids that are good at it. In fact, if we just brought back child labor, we wouldn't have to worry about educating everyone, and we wouldn't have to listen to people like Mr. Kozol anymore. Besides, having kids work builds their character.

The Best Education Money Can Buy

If you got through public schools and actually got your high school diploma, you now qualify to work at Wal-Mart, McDonalds, or any other low wage job. That's the American dream: to work for an American corporation such as Enron with long time job prospects. Congress and the President know that higher education is important and that it keeps America strong. They wave the flag and point out that anyone who wants to go to school can do so by using grants and loans. However, helping out with loans and granting money for school interferes with our tax cuts, and that would hurt the economy.

We're not cruel, so we didn't cut all the Pell Grants and loans to students. What we didn't want to do was to help too many undeserving people go to school. How would you know who deserved Pell Grants if you let everyone into college? As you know by now, giving money to the poor for school is just like throwing money down the toilet, and we should just cut college aid. These grants also create a dependency of the poor on the government.

A Patriot's Guide to Right-Wing Thinking

In 2005, 1.3 million students had Pell Grant moneys cut 13% and another 90,000 had the grants cut entirely. President Bush also froze the dollar amount of the Pell Grants at $4,500 a year (CNN.com). Congress gets a raise every year, but why should college students? These students have yet to do anything valuable for our country to deserve our help. If they can't afford college, they don't need college. This way, America will remain number one.

Another way we are keeping out the PLOWS is through tuition hikes all over the country. We cut the grants, and schools raised the tuition costs. Billionaires can afford high tuition, so it's okay to raise the average cost of universities.

Thirteen states returned tuition surveys for a study on rate increases. They all reported tuition increases. The increases included 2.4% at Michigan State and Wayne State (Michigan), and 19.8% at UT Arlington. According to the data, California and Arizona are the winners with nearly a 40% increase in tuition. Go team! Maybe costly tuition is why UC Berkeley teams are called the "Golden Bears".

Ivy League schools are out of reach unless you're a genius like Steven Hawking, theoretical physicist, or your daddy can help you get in like President Bush who went to Yale. For most, you have to be willing to take on tens of thousands of dollars of debt and be smart to get into a top-notch university. We should close all of those community colleges in America that our kids don't use. We have the universities.

TUITION HIKES
Sampling of state college tuition increases (for in-state full-time students), between 2002-3 and 2003-4 academic years:

• Univ. of Michigan: up 6.5%

• Ohio State: up 14.3%

• Univ. of Alabama: up 16.25%

• Univ. of Virginia: up 19%

• Iowa State: up 22.3%

• Univ. of Oklahoma: up 27.7%

• Univ. of Arizona: up 39%

• Univ. of California: up 39.4%

Source: NASULGC
National Association of State Universities and Land-Grant Colleges

---

Head Start—at stealing your money

Head Start is yet another national program of handouts. The program provides education, medical care, dental care, and food assistance for poor preschool children three to five years of age from low-income families. Once again, we're spending money on people that caused their own problems. These kids are to blame if their parents don't have enough money for childcare and are single mothers. We shouldn't have to pay for kids who are already used to ignorance and hunger. Instead of using our hard-earned tax dollars educating the poor, they could just use the television to baby-sit.

Head Start and Family Literacy say they are early education programs to help kids. Liberals say that an early education, like Head Start offers, is essential to kids when they get to elementary school. If liberals say Head Start is good, it must be bad. Again, they want to "throw money at the problem". There is no evidence that Head Start leads children to become Representatives, Senators, Presidents, lobbyists, corporate lawyers or heads of Fortune 500 companies, so we shouldn't waste money on it.

Vouchers and School Choice

Billionaires' kids should have an advantage because they are guaranteed to contribute to the wealth of this great nation. School choice means that if you're rich, you go to the school of your choice. Therefore, we're for it. We like vouchers because it allows us to get discounts on private schools, yet the value of each voucher is low enough to keep out the unclean children of the lower classes.

The greatness of grading, exit and entrance exams, testing, prayer in school, the Pledge of Allegiance, the Ten Commandments and other educational visual aids, along with home schooling (for us, not hippies, God forbid) can not be overestimated. For example, tests are a great way to separate the PLOWs from our future high-income children. It helps us and saves poor children time, allowing them to get on with their low wage careers.

There's Something Wrong with You, Now Go Shopping

One reason people are poor is how they consume; they don't consume enough. We are a consumer society, and we do everything to protect the consumer. We protect consumers by making sure that working Americans don't do anything so treasonous as to ask for a raise in the minimum wage. A raise in the minimum wage would lead to inflation and hurt consumers. Why do working people insist on a living wage when it would hurt consumers and lead to poverty, or at least a reduction in the number of PlayStations sold? Send these people off to Cuba if they despise consumers and America so much.

Consumer debt in the United States expanded 4.1 percent or $6 billion in July 2006, according to Federal Reserve statistics (Federal Reserve Bank). The Fed said that credit card, auto loan, and other non-mortgage personal debt totaled $1.77 trillion in July. By the end of 2006, consumer debt had reached over $2.4 trillion.

Consumers spend trillions of dollars in the United States every year, much of that at Christmas. Consumers are so important to creating wealth and getting out of poverty, that they have been protected in several ways:

- Bankruptcy laws have been passed to *protect consumers* against predatory bankruptcy laws.
- Minimum wage has been kept at a minimum to keep inflation down *for consumers* and create more wealth while reducing poverty.
- Jobs have been sent overseas to keep prices low on consumer goods, reducing poverty and *protecting consumers*.
- Mercury standards in our water supply have been relaxed to keep energy prices low *for consumers* and thus helping the poor.
- Canadian pharmaceuticals have been stopped at the border to prevent dangerous Canadian socialist medicines from infecting our population and hurting the poor struggling U.S. drug companies. Thus, *consumers are protected* against socialism and the poor are safe to spend more for their drugs.
- Many schools have protected the future of our economy by allowing advertising in school classrooms and hallways. By creating a fresh batch of consumers early on, the demand for products is higher, and prices for these products stay low.
- We've reduced safety regulations at amusement parks to keep the cost of entry into the Magic Kingdom low *for consumers*.
- Tort reform protects corporations from accident-prone citizens and keeps prices low *for consumers*.
- Credit card reform was passed to protect against predatory spending.

It has become clear that some of you aren't doing your patriotic duty and spending your heart out, even though if you consumed more you could be more. Well, let me tell those liberals out there that it is the role of all warm-blooded Americas to spend. If you know someone who lives within their means or sticks to a budget, it is your duty to make sure that their consumption increases.

There are ways to do this. First, show off your conspicuous consumption and laugh at them if they don't have 800 television channels, high-speed internet, I-pods with ports in every room, I-phones, and a luxury Lexus SUV. If they have kids, make sure to invite them over to play with your X-Box, Play Station 3, Nintendo Wii, Game Cube and most expensive high-speed computer to play games online. Let them see your Blackberry, and let them watch the Star Wars movies from your blu-ray discs played on your surround sound hi-definition system. Do anything to get them addicted to consuming.

Why You're Poor, and Why it's Your Fault

If all else fails, make sure that your friends and neighbors feel inadequate, and get them into the shopping spirit. Get them to buy more make-up, receive liposuction, use Viagra, and steroids, buy mood pills, or eat sugary foods to make themselves feel better. Then they're on their way to conspicuous consumption, and America thanks you.

Consumer spending now accounts for two-thirds of the U.S. economy, so if consumers pull back, the effect will be felt immediately. Commies want to take away our right to a decent standard of living. Don't let them do it. Keep spending. It's the only way to defend liberty and freedom. In President Bush's speech on September 20, 2001, he told us to just go on with our lives and keep spending (Wallace-Wells). All this spending has made us safe from terrorism.

You aren't spending enough. If you did, you would be able to save more money. What you need to do is drink more, see more movies, and just spend more. Otherwise, corporate profits will go down and we'll have to lay people off. You don't think we'd cut our multi-million dollar yearly salaries, do you?

Everyone can make it in America if they work hard. Forest Whitaker, award-winning actor, proved that with his Oscar acceptance speech, "It is possible for a kid from east Texas, raised in South Central L.A. in Carson (neighborhood), who believes in his dreams, commits himself to them with his heart, to touch them, and to have them happen (Billington)." If you just commit to your dreams and work hard, you too can become a rich Oscar winning actor. There is no need to fix the system at all. The problem with the poor is the poor themselves.

Chapter IV

God is Our Copilot

Abraham Lincoln, the 16th President of the U.S of A., once said that the question was not whether God was on our side but whether we were on God's side. Lincoln was wrong, and today he'd be drummed out of the Republican Party for such thoughts. He'd also be kicked out of the GOP for stealing property (slaves) from the poor beleaguered plantation owners.

God should work for us; He is my instrument, not the other way around. God is an instrument used to force the fear of gays into homes that previously never watched one episode of *Will and Grace*. God helps us eliminate welfare and Medicaid for millions and he sheds light on how we can blame job-stealing immigrants for unemployment.

God is everywhere. God is our guiding light and our tool. We use God to keep our country great. But most of all, we use God to get what we want and keep those we fear, our enemies, down. God is the guiding light that leads average Americans to distrust each other. Therefore, He is on the side of the elites. Religion divides people up into the holier then thou camp and the sinners because they're tolerant camp. The Republicans, along with God, use this divide to get votes for the party of true believers.

We give a special thanks to Jim Wallis (<u>God's Politics: Why the Right Gets It Wrong and the Left Doesn't Get It</u>) for being able to teach the heathen liberals that God has to be part of politics. No one, I mean no one, can be moral without God in his lives. On the flip side, you can do whatever you want as long as you are God fearing.

We like that our friends and allies moralize in the name of God because it helps us get richer. If Tom Delay, former speaker of the house, takes bribes, it's only to increase jobs for the military contractors who suffer under Bush. If Pat Robertson calls for the murder of democratically elected Hugo Chavez, it's because Chavez gives oil to the American poor at low prices. Therefore, his killing is justified to defend oil profits that are astoundingly low.

It's okay if conservatives like Gingrich have affairs and violate ethics and government security rules as long as they bow to the same God as the religious right. Newt Gingrich served his first wife with divorce papers when she was in the hospital for cancer treatments to save her the trouble of having to get out of bed (Scheer). We love Ronnie Reagan even though he was divorced because he fought commies for America. As long as you loathe gays, are against abortion under any circumstances, and are willing to give everything to God and the religious right, you can do whatever you want.

Jim Wallis got it right when including God in politics, but he should have left some things out. He makes a good argument that God must be in politics, but why does he mention this "God of inclusion"? We Billionaires, and our allies in Washington, D.C. promote the God of exclusion. God needs to be used to keep people in line, not to include people in decision-making. Radical Muslim clerics in some countries got it right by creating theocracies, although they obviously chose the wrong God (our God keeps kicking their God's ass).

Our God lets us dictate morality. And because we are more worthy, we can forgive, and damn, selectively. For example, if a liberal slept with a farm animal, it would be a grievous sin. However, if Republican anti-abortion activist Neal Horsley had sex with a mule, which he announced on the Alan Colmes Fox News Radio show on May 5, 2006, it's okay (POAC). Here's a transcript of the event found on the old American Century/White Rose Society message boards:

> At first, Horsley laughed and said, "Just because it's printed in the media, people jump to believe it."
> "Is it true?" Colmes asked.
> Hey, Alan, if you want to accuse me of having sex when I was a fool, I did everything that crossed my mind that looked like I...
> AC: You had sex with animals?
> NH: Absolutely. I was a fool. When you grow up on a farm in Georgia, your first girlfriend is a mule.
> AC: I'm not so sure that that is so.
> NH: You didn't grow up on a farm in Georgia, did you?
> AC: Are you suggesting that everybody who grows up on a farm in Georgia has a mule as a girlfriend?
> NH: It has historically been the case. You people are so far removed from the reality...

Having sex will animals, a mule in this case, is okay if you're an anti-abortionist and have given yourself to God. He was just demonstrating the figurative screwing of the Democrats by Republicans by literally screwing a mule. He was also demonstrating great love of animals that so many liberals accuse conservatives of not having. So get off our backs you liberals! You talk about how we hate animals and how meat is murder, but when a Republican shows true love for a beautiful member from the animal kingdom, it's a problem?

Conservatives have been charged and convicted of lots of sexual deviance, but it doesn't matter. If it weren't for all the sex on television, our beloved conservatives would never have been tempted to act out. The real difference in these conservative actions and that of regular people is that the conservatives caught in these sex scandals would never forgive others for the way they themselves acted. Therefore, conservatives are above reproach.

Because they use God to moralize about sex and family values, the conservatives cannot be criticized for their actions, no matter what they do. Plus, they all support Bush and take Jesus as their savior, and that forgives all sins. What few people understand is that you do not have to be moral to moralize. In fact, being moral gets in the way of moralizing.

Sanctity of Marriage, Republican Style

Republicans are for supporting traditional marriage just like they support education, democracy, and the American worker. Former President and conservative standard-bearer Ronald Reagan, the hero to many Republicans, divorced the mother of two of his children to marry Nancy Reagan. Nancy bore Reagan a daughter only <u>seven months</u> after the marriage. Perhaps because I don't want to know anything about biology, I thought a child needed <u>nine months</u> to incubate. That's okay, because at least he was married when he died, so Reagan's going to heaven.

Republican Congressmen divorce all the time, but they still know that God is on our side. Senator Bob Dole divorced the woman who got him through his WWII war wounds. That's what wives are for. He also does the Viagra ads to let us know that even *he* can get a woody. Now that's family values.

Republican Dick Armey, former House Majority Leader was divorced, former Senator Phil Gramm of Texas, Senator Lauch Faircloth, Alfonse D'Amato of New York, a Catholic nonetheless, fellow Catholic and Republican Senator Susan Molinari of New York, and the famous Senator John McCain of Arizona have all been divorced.

McCain divorced to marry his mistress. Neil Bush, President George W. Bush's brother, was also divorced along with several prominent Republican Governors such as John Engler of Michigan, Pete Wilson of California, and George Allen of Virginia. Remember, it was gay marriage that caused all of these divorces. Besides, liberals keep tempting us by keeping divorce legal in this country, so it's not our fault.

Mayor Rudy Giuliani was divorced twice, although he is Catholic. Rush Limbaugh and his wife Marta have shared vows of "til death do us part" six times between them. Other divorcees of note include former Secretary of State and hero Henry Kissinger.

None of this would matter whatsoever if it weren't for the liberals harping on about conservatives and the sanctity of marriage. It's the liberals that want to hurt marriage by allowing gays to marry. We want to ban gay marriage and promote flag burning amendments. We're on the moral high ground here. How dare liberals try to politicize the marital problems of good Americans. As we have learned, Republicans are so pro-family that many of them have started more than one.

When Bush's people and the Republican congressional leaders tell us that huge cuts in working family programs are needed to reduce the federal deficit and pay for Gulf Coast hurricane recovery, who are we to question? So what if the Bush tax cuts for the wealthy exceed the spending cuts and add to the federal deficit? It's all the tax and spend Democrats' fault that the budget gets out of control.

We all know that the Republicans, led by the conservative right, are for families, and so is God. Where there is a true God, your family will thrive. Let's look at the issues that are important to families.

First off, families need two parents: one man, one wife. Where there is only one parent, two men, or two wives or some other unnatural combination, God has abandoned them and they are forsaken. They are sinning. We cut programs that help single parents in order to help families. We also want to increase the tax cut for two-parent households. Self-reliant families who pray to God and don't ask for their taxes to be invested in schools are what keep America strong.

Republicans Give Hands-on Support to Kids

You might think that education and the war are the only ways Bush and his friends support families. Well you're wrong. Republicans are way into kids. I can hear our enemies use that one to bring out their list of Republican pedophiles. These poor victims of liberal attacks in the media are good God-fearing people. These Republicans accidentally let their urges get the better of them. Like Catholic priests, they have been moved on to greener pastures. These so-called Republican pedophiles have their seats guaranteed in heaven because they support President Bush and abhor gays, abortionists, and liberals. Besides, there are Democratic pedophiles. However, a Democrat's worst crime is

God is Our Copilot

not supporting President Bush in everything he wants. They should be spanked like the bad boys and girls they are.

Now remember, under Bush rules, you're guilty until proven innocent, at least as a terrorist. On the other hand, if you support Bush, you're never guilty. You'd only be guilty of loving our great country too much. As you read this, tell yourself that this is the word of God speaking through our party of the religious right and that it's God's will. We get the votes of the Christians because God loves us better than He loves the liberals. Keep voting Republican and you too can be holy like us.

Just because Republican Mayor Philip Giordano is serving a thirty-seven year sentence in federal prison for sexually abusing eight and ten-year old girls doesn't mean that he can't be right when he says gays are immoral. Republican hero and United States Senator Strom Thurmond liked to call blacks "blackies", and he wanted to keep segregation going into the next century. Therefore, when he had sex with a fifteen-year old black girl and made a baby, he was just trying to understand the black experience. He learned better then most why blacks should be separate from whites.

Republican congressman and anti-gay activist Robert Bauman was charged with having sex with a sixteen-year old boy he picked up at a gay bar. Even a Christian like Mr. Bauman was tempted by the boy who was on a recruiting mission from the gay cabal in the United States. Republican director of the "Young Republican Federation" Nicholas Elizondo molested his six-year old daughter who was possessed by the devil and tempted him. He was sentenced to six years in prison. All these facts are brought to you by the liberal traitors at <u>Republican Hypocrisy Revealed</u>. Why they need to give aid and comfort to the terrorists by revealing these state secrets is beyond me.

It's the devil and gays tempting good Republicans to act this way. Otherwise, how could the Republican Party have so many abusive members? Only a few dozen Republican leaders, as far as we know, have been involved in pedophilia. That doesn't mean that they are immoral and wrong about what they say. If you love America, you will see how the Republicans have cornered the market on morality.

It is God's will to make the friends of Bush richer every day. So support Bush, decry the heathens, call liberals names, and you too can be without sin. Anyway, these men live with different rules because they've done so much to help America.

War On Christmas

Rich Scarborough and the Christians of the Good Book at *Vision America* in Virginia tell us that there's a "war on Christians" in this country. They're right, by Jesus. Look at the venom people have for Christmas.

First, Christmas symbols and greetings are being purged. Workers at Target stores are banned from saying "Merry Christmas" and have to use the Christ hating "happy holidays". Why does Target insult Christians so much? They must be pandering to the Jews who are so into shopping and selling. I hear you can't even enter a synagogue and wish people "Merry Christmas" anymore.

Judges banned "one nation under God" from the Pledge of Allegiance. Don't the judges trust God? They really must despise Christians if they want to take God out of the Pledge. We created all that fear of communism in the 1950s to get "one nation under God" put in the Pledge of Allegiance.

Judges have removed Ten Commandments monuments from public buildings. If we remove them, the buildings won't be protected from Godless terrorists. There has also been a call for an end to religious expression, by stifling prayer, at the Air Force Academy. Shouldn't pilots be allowed to pray as a group and force everyone to pray to the same God so that we are all protected from terrorists?

Christians were arrested for praying at a "gay pride" rally in Philadelphia. Our interference with their constitutionally protected rally was only to save the souls of sinners. Gays did get homosexual "marriage" in Massachusetts and California. Why should they feel that they should have freedom of religion when they so clearly have shown how they disobey God?

Hollywood once again shows that they support the anti-Christ by putting the satanic Da Vinci Code into theaters. Any alternative view of religion shows that Hollywood blasphemes God. That includes the elfin religion shown in the Lord of the Rings movies. That goes more than double for the Harry Potter movies; there are seven of those and only three *Rings* movies (Berkowitz).

The apocalyptic cult of Christians will rise up so we can raise money to get our men elected. As French playwright Jean Anouilh once said, "Every man thinks God is on his side. The rich and powerful know he is." True, so true. God is on our side. That leads us to the original rich Americas, the founding fathers.

The Founding Fathers: As Religious as We Want Them to Be

The founding fathers, Jefferson, Madison, Franklin, and Adams were religious. They wanted a theocracy in the United States. We like to talk about how the founding fathers were religious so that we can show how God has always guided us. There is a God, and God wanted us to invade Iraq. God is on our side; we created Him, and we use *Him* to attack other countries. According to Pastor Rick Scarborough:

> The left will continue to accuse us of trying to 'Christianize America.' Because it can't debate us on the issues, it seeks to demonize us. But we are the inheritors of the faith tradition that is part of the fabric of America. We seek to return America to the Godly values espoused by leaders like Washington, Adams, Lincoln and Reagan. And we have just as much right to be actively involved in the political process as other citizens (Berkowitz).

So apparently, the founding fathers were really religious, and we know that because Mr. Scarborough says so. If you were counting, Scarborough mentioned Washington, Adams, Lincoln, and Reagan but left out Jefferson, Franklin, Thomas Paine, and Madison, among others. Why? I don't know. They really were Christians though.

Let's look at Jefferson, the main writer for the Declaration of Independence. He believed in God so much that he only mentioned Him once in the document. However, that didn't mean he wanted Him out of our government, did it? He liked the Bible so much he cut one up to make his own version (Morgan). He even had a bit of a Jesus complex when he said, "I am a sect unto myself" (ibid).

Jefferson questioned the existence of God like all good Christians. Jefferson once said, "No nation has ever yet existed or been governed without religion". That proves he supported religion. Just as Lincoln supported killing when he said, "No war ever existed without killing" and doctors support disease when they say, "Man is not without disease". Jefferson wanted freedom of religion, and that meant religion should rule everyone with government as God's chariot. Only the religion that supports the rich should rule. I'm sure that is what Jefferson would have wanted, just like I'm sure that Bush knew what God wanted when he invaded Iraq.

James Madison, architect of the Constitution, was a forgetful man. That is why he didn't put God in the Constitution. He forgot. I am sure there were post-it notes on his desk that reminded him, "write Article 8 to the Constitution that talks about God being the best", but he misplaced it. When Madison denounced the presence of Chaplains in Congress, it was not because he didn't want them in Congress (ibid). He was denouncing them for not visiting him at home. When Madison complained about the power of the church in America, he was just jealous that he didn't have such power.

Madison wanted religion in government, he was just too jealous to admit it. As Joseph Loconte wrote of Madison for the Heritage Foundation, a non-partisan group if I ever knew one, in his article "Why Religious Values Support American Values" (Loconte), Madison "came to regard freedom of conscience as a sacred right and a binding political obligation." And as we know, "freedom of conscience" is the same thing as "freedom of religion" which is the same thing as "it is your political duty to put religion in your government." Amen brother!

John Adams was a Unitarian, which proves how much he believed in Jesus Christ. So what if Unitarians don't force their congregation to pledge a belief in a Christian god. What does that have to do with Adams? He was against hypocrisy and mysticism, which meant he didn't like Islam. Moreover, he supported the use of religion for war when he said, "As I understand the Christian religion, it was, and is, a revelation. But how has it happened that millions of fables, tales, and legends, have been blended with both Jewish and Christian revelation that have made them the bloodiest religion that ever existed?" (Morgan). So you see, we're right to use religion to kill, and that comes from John Adams himself. All the Biblical stories mixed together makes the religion bloody, i.e. a conduit for spilling the blood of heathens. Onward Christian soldiers!

Talking Points for God, or How to Shut Up them Liberals

There are lot of terrorist-supporting atheists and agnostics who want to tell you about the separation of church and state and how important it is to keep God out of the government. Here are some talking points for those of you who want to keep on supporting the side of God, America and its leaders.

Why do we say "One nation under God" in the Pledge of Allegiance if religion isn't in government? So what if the pledge was around nearly forty years before that line about God was added because of the second communist scare (see chapter I). That doesn't mean that God didn't want it in from the start.

In America, we have "in God we trust" written on our money. We added the phrase to our coins after the Civil War. Paper money didn't have "In God We Trust" on it until 1957. My God, the heathens! No God on our money.

How did we survive? They used to have this liberal message on it, "From many, One". Liberals will use this to tell us that God wasn't meant to be on our money or in our government. If you want to get liberals to stop talking about facts and all, do what Bill O'Reilly does when liberals use facts he doesn't like: tell them to "SHUT UP!"

If we aren't a Christian nation, why do oaths for President and other offices end with, "so help you God"? Just because it wasn't in the original oath doesn't mean that the first presidents weren't Christian. The liberals would just misunderstand that. If you remember your history the way we want, God was always running this government.

In case you haven't seen how I proved it thus far: this nation was founded on religion. In fact, if it hadn't been for religious persecution in Europe, especially England, North America might never have been colonized. That is why it is imperative that we look to religion to keep us number one.

We Love Armageddon!

Fundamental Christians have a built in fear mechanism that keeps them the best; it's called Armageddon. The rich folk like Armageddon because it makes the poor and religious useful in the battle against democratic evil.

End-of-days cultists have lots to fear: gays, sex, free thinkers, liberals, non-Christians (see the Fear-O-Matic, chapter I) and we can get them to vote for any candidate that fears God as they do. This creates what I like to call the *Great Circle of Fear*. The more you fear, the more likely you are to join a fundamentalist religion. The more fundamental religion you get, the more you fear, the more you fear, the more you go to the fundamentalist Church and read the fundamentalist Bible, the more you fear, and so on. All we have to do is join a Christian church and preach about these fears, and there are millions of votes lining up for us.

Now remember, not all Churches promote fear like they should, so make sure that you go to the firebrand fundamentalist kind. Let's not forget our friends at the Catholic League, the Catholic fundamentalist organization headed by President William A. Donohue. They help us because so many of them are pro-life, pro-death penalty, *and* anti-birth control. It's believers like that who keep us in power and invading heathen countries, in God's name of course.

Dr. Paul Cameron, a scientist often quoted by religious right groups, speaking at the 1985 Conservative Political Action Conference said, "Unless we get medically lucky, in three or four years, one of the options discussed will be the extermination of homosexuals" (hatecrime.org). But Mr. Cameron

Church
Bible
fear   **Bible**   **Church**
Church   fear   **fear**
                    Bible
fear   church   fear   **Bible**
Bible   **Bible**   **fear**
     fear   **Church**

is wrong in America? They are so easy to scapegoat because there's so much fear of them in America. By bringing up gay marriage and blogging gay hate, the gay hating folk feel comfortable voting for our politicians.

You Can Never Be Too Paranoid

William Donahue, when asked about television shows that featured Catholicism, said:

> There's no easier target in the United States in 2006 than the Catholic Church. It's partly because the church itself has been delinquent in its handling of the sexual abuse scandal and partly because there is a strong strain of bigotry in our society [among people] who receive bad news about the Catholic Church as good news (Donaldson-Evans).

That proves that there is a movement against the Catholic Church. We love William Donohue because he knows how to see a criticism of himself or the

Church as proof that the whole world is against Catholics. He speaks volumes every time someone criticizes the Catholic Church.

He has his own website for the Catholic League, promotes boycotts of films and corporations, and works politically to get anti-gay measures and candidates on the ballot. He is a champion for us all because he is so far removed from reality—poverty, killing, war, hunger, and corporate crimes—that he can focus on his own persecution. He is another lynchpin in the war of our truth against their facts, and we salute him.

Pro-life: The Gift that Keeps on Giving

A special salute goes out to the Catholics who don't like abortion or allow birth control. Praise Jesus! This two-pronged attack to save life keeps the abortion issue at the top of the agenda in national, state, and local elections.

By prohibiting parishioner access to birth control and condoms (especially in Africa), the Catholic Church increases the number of pregnancies. Moreover, these Catholics can't have abortions, so this leads to more poverty. People that are more desperate seek the kind words of the Catholic Church, where they learn to have more children no matter how many die of starvation. More children means more Catholics; therefore, more children have children because they don't know about birth control. Using birth control is a sin, you see. What a great Catholic perpetuating machine.

Current and former Popes have a special place in the minds and hearts of every African who dies of AIDS because they had no condoms and all the hungry Latin Americas who can't stop their hot blood from boiling over and having sex. At least they have kids instead of using birth control, so they will not be going to hell. Thanks to Popes banning birth control, there are more pregnancies, and there are more people in Africa with AIDS because we can't send condoms overseas. God forbid.

Here's where America benefits from the Pope and people like William Donohue who are so against birth control and abortion. More Catholics means a larger pool of low-wage workers coming from Catholic dominated Mexico to the U.S. It also leads to the heated immigrant debate and increased profits for our companies that run border security. The abortion issue helps the Right get elected and make money. It keeps wages low and gives us the Mexicans to fear and scapegoat. You've got to love the abortion debate.

As stated earlier in the book, liberals are baby killers. They are against life and are pro-abortion. Liberals think abortion is an easy thing for women and that it is a fun recreational sport, kind of like Vice President Cheney shooting quail.

We don't like abortion because we hate to enjoy sex. If we enjoyed sex, we would go to hell. Look at me, Tex Shelters. I don't have sex, and I sleep with a Colt 45 under my pillow and a safe full of money over my head. Therefore, I am against abortions.

There are a huge number of abortions each year, about 1.3 million in the United States (Associated Press). Women of childbearing age are having sex about ninety-one times a year (ibid). Let's call it ninety. The United States Census Bureau says there were 61,577,297 females between fifteen and forty-four, the "childbearing years" (Census). Take out 8.6% who call themselves gay and that leaves 56,281,506 women having sex ninety times a year, which would be 5,065,348,451 number of sex, acts by women.

Even though men can't have an abortion, I thank all you males for fighting the good fight against choice. Of over 5 billion sex acts in the United States every year, there were an outrageous 1,300,000 abortions. That's .03% abortions from a sex act, and there is a dangerous three in ten thousand chance a sex act will lead to an abortion. Just stop having sex America!

As you know, you have to be against abortion to be "pro-life" and if you are for a woman's right to choose, you are the "abortion lobby" that just wants to increase the number of abortions. If you support abortion, you're into killing. If you're against the war and pro-abortion, you're a baby killer. Remember, you can be *pro-life*, support the war in Iraq, and promote the death penalty.

Since Planned Parenthood came into being in the fifties, the number of abortions has increased; therefore, Planned Parenthood *caused* these abortions. We are wise to say so. The population of the United States is almost double the population of the 1950s when Planned Parenthood opened. Furthermore, people are more sexually active then ever before, and abortions are more available. There is also better record keeping to record the abortions that do occur. All the illegal back-alley abortions or the abortions a child gets when a rich daddy sends his daughter to Europe for an abortion are now legal and counted in the statistics.

All this might be true, but because Planned Parenthood records the abortions, they are responsible for the rise in abortions. In this case, we should kill the messenger. How dare Planned Parenthood help women stay out of poverty by allowing women to choose the right time to have a child.

Abortions are out of control, and we want to applaud the right-thinking men, and women, for their continued efforts to use the facts in a way that supports our beliefs. Women are out there just waiting to have abortions, and people are having them for fun. Please believe that there are doctors out their just drooling at the chance to kill a baby. When we convince the pro-fetus right-wing folks that pro-choice liberals like abortions, it's easier for us to get the votes we need to control Congress and control the feminazis. Then we get to stand on the moral high ground.

Liberals will lie and say that no one actually likes abortions, and that abortions are used to help women at risk of dying during pregnancy. Understanding that women make tough choices, and that they are thoughtful about abortion, loses us votes. Therefore, we must repeat the "baby killer", "pro-abortion", "anti-life", "God hating" name calling against liberals. It's working. If single women take babies to term, they're single welfare sluts; if they have an abortion, they're baby killers. Either way, they're wrong, and we're right.

Liberals make all sorts of excuses for women killing their babies using abortions. Researchers at the Association for Geographical Information survey (AGI) found that women chose abortions for many reasons, the top one being they are selfish sluts. However, none of the women would admit it in the survey.

Some women say they chose an abortion because they have health problems (12%). Others thought that possible fetal health problems were an excuse to have an abortion (13%). What does the health of the mother or the fetus have to do with terminating the pregnancy?

Many women said they were unready (32%). Some said they were too immature to have a baby (22%) or that they needed to finish their education first (34%). I say you're never too young or too uneducated to have a baby.

Women also said that they had problems with relationship and wanted to avoid single parenthood (48%). Being a single mother is not big deal. Just ask Harry Potter author JK Rowling, the richest women in England, how easy it is for her to raise a child as a single parent. If she can do it, anyone can.

Some mothers say they can't afford a baby now (73%). So? Just because some women say they had an abortion because they are unmarried (42%), can't afford basic life needs (23%), are unemployed (22%), or can't leave a job to care for a baby (21%) doesn't mean they can't afford to properly care for a baby (Finer, et al). The upshot of this is that women want to have a good life and be ready to give babies all the love and attention they need and deserve. If you ask me, that's just selfish.

Other People We Distain Because They're not Christian

Environmentalists are not our kind, and we dismiss Deists. Anyone making the environment real important is making it more important than God, and we don't like that type of idolatry. Jesus frowned upon idolatry, so were against environmentalists who make nature into their God. As long as we pray, that's all that's important. God will care for the environment. This allows all the rich corporations to go on polluting and getting rich. We don't like environmentalists because they create a false idol out of nature:

> Modern-day "environmentalism" often tends to be another counterfeit. Any form of "environmentalism" that places greater emphasis on *creation*, than on the *Creator*, or who values plants, rocks and animals more than they value human life, is a form of idolatry - a counterfeit "environmentalism".
>
> God has ultimate control over creation, and uses it to accomplish his purposes. This is the concept of "providence". Under normal conditions, he works *with* the "laws of nature" (which he created). But he has, at times, accomplished his purposes by overruling the "laws of nature" - and he has the right to do so (My Journal).

God has the right to change the laws of nature if He wishes, so if He wants global warming, it is heresy to complain about it.

We dislike these scientists who want to tell us what to do. Those global warming "experts" with their ideas about greenhouses don't know a thing. With former Clinton V.P. Al Gore on their side, there has got to be something wrong with that global warming crowd. Guilt by association is always a way to get at the truth.

If the planet is warming, it is only God's light that warms it. God's divine light shines through the billions of pounds of air pollutants dumped everyday in the United States. If there is global warming, it is God's will. Who are humans to say anything about pollution's place in God's plan?

Cutting pollution would mean rich folks would have to reduce the number of vacation homes and luxury automobiles we own. If we had to pay the costs our pollutants caused to our country, it would hurt. That in turn would hurt the economy and we'd have to lay off half our house staff and factory workers just to get over it. We'd have to sell one of our private jets.

Another thing we don't need is the Endangered Species Act (ESA). It's ungodly. God created all the beasts, and if he says humans should rule, who are we to question? As I am sure you understand by now because I told you, God has chosen the United States as his messenger and greatest nation.

The same is true for humans. We are God's chosen species; in fact, we are made in *His* image. Humans should rule the earth like God rules the heavens (so much for air pollution) and the devil rules the underworld. God has given us reign over the animals to eat and kill them as we wish even if it means torturing those animals like terrorist suspects. If God wants more species, he'll create some. We don't need the ESA at all.

We are against the ESA and other such laws because it hurts American workers just like we're against the Kyoto Protocol on greenhouse gas emissions too. We're against conserving trees because it hurts logging communities and takes away jobs. And don't let them liberal enviroterrorists tell you that the only way to keep jobs in the long run is to have a "conservation plan" for our forests.

What's wrong with the "greenhouse affect"? Plants thrive in greenhouses. Humans are just another species that will thrive in a greenhouse too. You can now safely drive your SUVs, use your aerosols, and eat as much factory farmed beef you want without guilt.

Evil Universities

Universities are hotbeds of sin. According to Allan Bloom, author of <u>The Closing of the American Mind</u>, university students today have no moral values because university professors teach students that there is no wrong or right and all morality is subjective. How does Bloom know this? He must have talked to all the professors in this country and even those at Oral Roberts, Regent University School of Law founded by televangelist Pat Robertson, Liberty University founded in 1971 by televangelist Jerry Falwell, and Ave Maria School of Law. Those are certainly hotbeds of liberal thought, just like Yale. It's a wonder Presidents Bush Jr. and Sr. survived such a liberal university as Yale.

There were only 185 religious universities listed on the internet when I looked. They must all be liberal as well. In addition, many four-year universities in America have religious studies programs and most have Young Republican clubs. However, there are more science programs than religious majors in the universities, and that is a disgrace. This shows how much religion is discriminated against in the United States.

We know that kids are forced to go to non-religious schools and that these kids have no choice but to be indoctrinated into liberalism. Liberals seem to think there are grey areas in the moral plane and that morals are subjective. In order to show how moral we are, we must force morals down the throats of these evil professors and kill them if they disagree.

The Ten Commandments

There are things we can do to ensure this country stays Christian. We must help others find the Lord Jesus as a savior. First, bring the Biblical Ten Commandments back into our courtrooms, schools, civic places, and other public spaces. If people see the Ten Commandments everywhere, people will be reminded not to kill, and the murder rate will go down.

Just seeing the Ten Commandments will be a deterrent to all sorts of bad behavior. They are helping Republicans stay moral. The commandments will also remind people not to covet wives and other things that aren't theirs. If we place the Ten Commandants everywhere, including above urinals in every truck stop in America, people will remember to behave morally.

We Value Family Values

We believe in families, as do the holy God-fearing masses. We believe so much in families that anyone who doesn't have children should get fewer tax cuts. If you don't have children and are over thirty, you're either gay or a communist (like the Chinese who passed laws to stop having so many kids), and you support terrorism.

We cut AFDC welfare payments to give single mothers a kick in the ass to get a job. We passed unemployment reform to ensure that workers think twice about leaving a job that they just don't like because it makes them sick. Why should these workers get fired from these good jobs then live off of the rest of us hardworking taxpayers for so long? We do all of this to help the families in America.

We prevent safe abortions for mothers in danger of dying during birth, and enforce mandatory sentencing for first time pot smokers for all the families. When we cut funding for Pell Grants for college, we're only helping you understand that education is not for every child. We wouldn't want you to have false hopes now would we? We protect families by keeping minimum wage low, thus keeping consumer prices down for all the Wal-Mart shoppers.

The war in Iraq is also good for families. Wars help get little Johnny and Mary out of the house and allow them the opportunity to explore new lands and meet new people, even if they might have to shoot them. Families couldn't help their kids do all that on minimum wage. And when your little darlings come back from Iraq, they will have money for school, if we still have any money left after the liberals in Congress get a hold of it.

God is Our Copilot

Education and other help come to those that do what we want at the risk of their lives. It's because we're all about the family. Families are the corner stone we build on top of, and profit from, every chance we get. Families are the foundation that keeps Billionaires, and thus our nation, prosperous.

I have proven yet again that God is our copilot. He works for us. He's on the side of the rich and powerful as they work and aid the poor in ways they never thought they could be helped. My favorite part is that some "liberal Christians", meaning not true Christians, are getting their jock straps into a knot over the idea that God has chosen us over them.

The Right is more Christian than anyone else is, and this helps keep our country great. We get people to vote on issues such as abortion, gays, and all types of morality issues. That leaves the economic issues in the hands of the business people who know how to make money. As long as people are concerned with moral issues, they will get into heaven. Leave your money to the corporations and us. In fact, let corporations run everything.

Chapter V

Corporations Should Run Everything

Corporations have done so much for this country, it's hard to list it all. Nevertheless, as true patriot, it is my duty to try. Corporations have created unending wealth for everyone; that *cannot* be argued. Corporations have also protected workers rights, human rights, and the environment. They have helped American families and promoted politics here and overseas. Corporations have created all the needed goods for our country. They have done all this and more despite the fact that government gets in the way of them doing what they need to do to keep this country great. As a Billionaire, I should know.

A corporation is a common form of legal business organization. It is especially useful for big businesses like the ones Billionaires own and run because it allows all sorts of people to invest and limits liability for the stockholders. States allow you to incorporate your business, and you can have your corporate charter as long as you want. It's a way to make lots of money and avoid responsibility.

As a corporation, you can influence the government like an individual. Moreover, a corporation has a lot more money to buy influence. As Joel Barkin, a liberal, admits in his book The Corporation, "They [corporations] determine what we eat, what we watch, what we wear, where we work, and what we do" (Barkin 5). Since that is true, and they're doing it so well, why shouldn't corporations run everything?

The Government is the Enemy

There is too much government interference in our lives. The government wants to not only control how and when you can shoot off your Colt 45 or M-16 (a sweet gun to shoot suckers), but they want to tell you when and where to take out your trash and tell you how much you can drink before driving. The government also wants to tell businesses that they can't sell rotten meat, can't sell poisoned medicine, and that they have to allow workers to take toilet brakes and eat lunch.

If people want to buy poisoned meat or bad medicine, carry guns into schools, drive on unsafe roads, smoke toxic cigarettes, sleep in unsafe hotels, or eat rat turds in their cereal every morning, why should the government interfere? The government should get involved in some things; for example, telling people whom they can or can't sleep with and how women should run their bodies—like baby machines. Just insert, and out comes a baby.

However, the only institution that has been there for America from the beginning is the corporation. Therefore, corporations should run everything, and the government and the people should step aside. Corporations should be allowed to make profit free of interference, and the marketplace should rule. There is a lot corporations could fix if the government would just get out of the way, and in this chapter, I tell you how.

The History of Helpful Corporations

A corporation's individual rights were not recognized at the beginning of the United States even though it was the corporations that helped England successfully colonize North America. New Hampshire even revoked the corporate charter of Dartmouth College. That was probably because they were teaching kids about evolution, and the government had the sense back then to keep evolution down. In fact, there is very little discussion of evolution in the 18th Century. That shows how God fearing the American folk were.

The unenlightened Colonists required corporations to renew their charters every few years. Thankfully, we now just give corporations a pass no matter what they do. In the past, corporations' democratic rights were taken away, and they weren't allowed to be involved in the electoral process. The Supreme Court even affirmed a state's power over corporations in Dodge v Woolsey (1855). That decision guaranteed that corporations had to endure the terrible fate of getting their rights *after* blacks got theirs. At least corporations got rights before women got the vote.

Business started America and made it great. Without colonial corporations, labor would not have made its way from Africa to the Americas. Millions of Africans would not have been liberated and basketball, jazz and fried chicken would not be as popular today if it wasn't for this migration of workers from Africa. Just ask Ann Coulter or Ayn Rand of the importance of unrestrained free enterprise (in slaves) to the growth of freedom (slavery). They know the truth, and they prove that women can also be compassionate conservatives.

Other than African immigration, corporations have helped America in many ways. Therefore, the government and the people should give corporations whatever they desire.

- Corporations and the wealthy helped win the American Revolutionary War, the Civil War, World War I and II, and the United States is still gloriously and successfully in a state of war only because of corporations.

- They helped basketball players and other sports players make millions because of corporations selling shoes and beer.
- They helped CEOs earn millions laying off workers and thus helping the United States remain a low-income nation.
- Corporations made health care a success for everyone with HMOs and insurance companies helping with national health care.
- Congress functions properly because it is always obeying the whims of corporations.
- We have a society that donates to the poor more than any other nation because eating and having a home is an option based on charity in the United States. We can choose who the deserving people are and who aren't, just like Jesus Christ would have.
- We have a pool of reserve labor that is easily exploited.
- We have the best President and Congress money can buy.

If corporations ran everything there would be less government waste. Every dollar of waste is an abomination, and if an agency wastes one dollar, I say *one dollar*, that agency should be eliminated. So, bye bye welfare, Medicare, Medicaid, the Department of Education, Interior, HUD, Labor and all those other department and programs set up to help average citizens. Governments waste money on problems aimed to help lazy folks. Only lazy folks get food stamps, so cut that program out. Military spending is never a waste because it costs money to kill people. I prove all of that in this chapter.

The Beginning

North America was discovered after the corporation was already established in England. Boatloads of Brits came over to America with corporate thinking. The corporate form was used for plantations and towns, for charitable, religious, literary foundations, trading, and local business purposes. Corporations made the British number one and made the Colonies great as well. If any of them liberals tell you it was hard working people and not corporations that made this country prosperous, they are just lying, America hating commies.

Christianity was here early in the colonies, and we formed our government based on religion as we learned in chapter four. Corporations were here early, so they should run everything too. In fact, without corporations, North America would never have been settled. That proves they should make all the decisions for everyone.

Sir Walter Raleigh colonized Virginia with a corporation and got everyone to start smoking tobacco. This smoking made us great in the early days. Corporations in Jamestown and Plymouth created the first two English settlements. Corporations invested in the colony and that helped them buy guns and plow land. Straight shooting and pork barreling became early enterprises in the soon to be United States. They still are today.

The other colonies were founded by corporate investment and free trade. We should be eternally grateful to the corporate state and give our lives to it. We should work only for God, corporation and country. Working for people, family, and community is a treasonous heresy that gives aid and comfort to the terrorists. The biggest problem is that the government keeps getting in the way.

Government Jealousy

Corporations were running things before the revolution, but the new United States government was jealous and took away the rightful power of the corporations. The founding fathers, religious and all as they were, were confused. They didn't give corporations all they wanted, and that means corporations didn't get what they needed to help this country be great. The lawmakers kept the corporations down for over one hundred years after the revolution (ReclaimDemocracy.org).

At the start, corporate charters were limited and the government could revoke charters if the corporations violated laws. So what if corporations violate laws. I'm sure they do it to defend workers. Corporations shouldn't have their licenses revoked even if they do break the law. Not even law and order Republicans would be that cruel.

Corporations were limited to doing business and making money but were kept from the necessary corporate activities such as investing in politicians, subsidizing the police, and financing other public officials. Corporations couldn't own stock in other corporations nor own any property that did not pertain to their chartered purpose. This meant that they couldn't merge with another company as a way to get rid of unnecessary labor. They were terminated if they hurt people. Isn't terminating a corporation hurting people?

Owners and managers of corporations were responsible for criminal acts that workers committed on the job. What were they thinking by making the owners responsible? How'd they expect corporations to make a living following these draconian laws?

Corporations could not make any political or charitable contributions nor spend money to influence law making. Individual Colonies also limited corporate charters to a set number of years because the states were full of commies back in the late 1700s and early 1800s. Corporations were having their rights taken away until the after the Civil War and 14th Amendment was passed and the cross-country expansion of the railway system was underway.

Corporations are People Too

The idea that "corporations are people" is one of the best, most enduring, most profitable ideas ever made up. Now, you can no longer sue the CEOs or owners (stockholders) of a corporation. You have to sue the corporations directly, and they have the rights of a person. Corporations now have the same legal protections as people: the right to a trial by jury, free speech, equal protection under the Fourteenth Amendment, the right to face your accusers, and so on.

Thanks to the hard work of the corporate-backed courts, Congress, and corporate lawyers (not all lawyers are blood sucking parasitic liberals), the idea of corporate personhood has endured from the 1890s to this day. Finally, the yolk of government and the people was off the backs of corporations. Now they can do what they do best, make enormous profits to benefit the nation. Remember, the only way to help workers is to give corporations whatever they want.

The Civil War was a great event for corporations. It was a time when U.S. corporations learned what a boom to business war is. There's no business like war business. Lincoln knew that we needed to keep the Union together in order to have the Southern exports and markets. The Civil War had to be won to assure Northern goods would be sold in the South and abroad. Pro-corporate laws and decisions after the Civil War paved the way for one of the most honest and hard working groups of capitalists ever, the robber barons.

The robber barons worked real hard to own a majority control of an industry in order to control prices. That way they could fairly undercut the competition, put them out of business, and then raise prices even higher to maximize profit.

The war helped speed up the development of the railroad in the United States, and that increased the power of the corporation in America. The Civil War was the first U.S. war that used railroads as a major means of military transport. This was a change from past wars when the soldiers had to travel on foot or horse, two modes of transit that didn't require huge amounts of capital that only corporations could afford. With the Civil War, corporations not only made money selling bullets, bombs, and bayonets, but they made money shipping the soldiers and supplies around on their railroads.

The end of the Civil War and Reconstruction brought an upswing in the fortunes of corporations. Then Congress passed a law that on one hand seemed to take away the power of corporations, and on the other hand gave them personhood: the Sherman Anti-trust act of 1890. Section 7 of the Sherman act gave people the right to sue corporations and section 8 finally recognized corporations as people:

> Sec. 7. Any person who shall be injured in his business or property by any other person or corporation by reason of anything forbidden or declared to be unlawful by this act, may sue therefore in any circuit court of the United States in the district in which the defendant resides or is found, without respect to the amount in controversy, and shall recover threefold the damages by him sustained, and the costs of suit, including a reasonable attorney's fee.
>
> Sec. 8. That the word "person," or "persons," wherever used in this act shall be deemed to include corporations and associations existing under or authorized by the laws of either the United States, the laws of any of the Territories, and the laws of any State, or the laws of any foreign country (US.gov 1).

Suddenly, states and governments had to recognize corporations as persons. This meant a lot of things, but best of all for us moneyed folks was that the government of the people couldn't pass laws that took away corporate rights. Any law that was passed to regulate corporations could be seen as a restriction of that corporation's right to equal protection under the Fourteenth Amendment. For example, the government couldn't regulate rail prices without going through a court procedure. This prevented the government from putting any limits on rail prices and allowed big profits for the railroad barons.

Corporate personhood also made it hard to control trusts. A trust is a way corporations can band together to control prices and markets without having to compete with each other. Forming a trust is a way corporations could claim "equal protection" under the Fourteenth Amendment; if workers can unite in unions, corporations as persons can unite in a trust.

However, the Sherman Act went too far and restricted corporations from owning other corporations. Thankfully, states stepped in. In 1890, New Jersey courts cut down the Sherman Act by allowing corporations to buy stock of another corporations and pay for this stock with their own stock. Suddenly, corporations could own each other through a control of their common stock.

New Jersey passed other laws in the 1890s allowing New Jersey corporations to merge and grant corporate charters to companies outside New Jersey's borders. This allowed companies all over the country to incorporate in New Jersey and supersede most antitrust provisions of the Sherman Act. This and other court decisions allowed more mergers *after* the Sherman Antitrust law was passed than ever before in history. Between 1830 and 1860, dozens of rail companies incorporated because of the government's public land give away to some sixty-one railroad companies (ReclaimDemocracy.org).

You might think that corporations allowed the average citizen to invest in railroads, and in a sense, it was true. That is the idea Bush tried promoted with the words "ownership society". Large shareholders control the boards of corporations and small shareholders go along for the ride. The large shareholders travel to, and influence, the stockholders meetings; the small shareholders don't. Even if small shareholders do show up, they don't have sway over the decisions of the board of directors or CEO. That is the way God intended.

The interests of the small and large shareholder are different. Small investors want to make dividends while large investors want to control companies and expand. Large investors will take short-term losses; small investors can't afford losses and might be forced to sell before stocks rise in value. This way, corporations can take advantage of small investors who front the corporations some money but don't reap the long-term benefits. Is it a surprise that few corporations give dividends today?

Delaware decided to give the corporations more "liberty and independence" (the state motto) in 1899 when they came up with the General Corporation Law. This law allowed the corporations to write regulations for themselves to follow. That's like the police passing laws that allow police to beat prisoners because it helps them get confessions. Delaware understood that corporations knew best how to regulate themselves because corporations know more about corporations than anybody else does. This is why DuPont moved their operations to Delaware for the benefit of everyone.

Between 1894 and 1905, unions tried to raise wages and reduce deaths of the railroad workers. However, court rulings stopped workers' needs from ruining the railroads. In 1894, the courts finally said that eight-hours shift for lazy mechanics and slacking off laborers was illegal and forced workers to work any number of hours corporations told them to work.

In 1895, filthy women garment workers had the eight-hour shifts they had won taken away in Ritchie versus People. Even bakers were trying to slack off and keep bread away from breadwinners by only working ten-hour days. However, in 1905, the Lochner versus New York court decision made the bakers' short ten-hour day illegal (ibid). There were other laws that made it illegal to strike. Even back in the late 1900s, people realized striking workers were a national security threat and gave aid and comfort to the terrorists. As we all know, laws to help workers have a life and a living wage are unpatriotic.

In 1976, the best decision ever by the courts, Buckley versus Valeo, was passed. As God had ordained in the Bible, the courts finally gave campaign contributions freedom of speech protection. Suddenly, the wise corporations could give money to campaigns without limit (ibid). This allowed corporations to support candidates without regulation. Republicans finally got a court wise enough to recognize the importance of defending money. Protecting money always protects workers.

Another corporate backed court decision in 1976 was U.S. versus Martin Linen Supply Co. The court ruled that corporations have Fifth Amendment protection against double jeopardy. Now courts can dismiss lots of frivolous lawsuits against corporations from people who can't read directions on their products. For example, if someone in Iowa lost a lawsuit against an asbestos maker, the corporation could be protected from further lawsuits in other states because it would constitute double jeopardy.

Later that year, the court ruled that advertising was free speech so corporations could make up all sorts of facts when they advertised in order to sell their products. This free speech ruling for advertising increased the number of facts corporations could spread to America to increase sales (ibid).

The following year, in Marshall versus Barlow, courts said OSHA (Occupation, Safety, and Health Administration) inspectors couldn't just show up and inspect the work place without a warrant. This protected companies against surprise inspections where inspectors might catch corporations doing sensitive work like hiding chemical spills and doctoring safety records. Keeping safety records safe helps us prevent terrorism because terrorists would attack unsafe industries if they knew about them.

Later that year, the court overturned state restrictions on corporate spending for political referendums. In First National Bank versus Bellotti, the court decided that First Amendment protections could be invoked. That ruling meant that money was now considered free speech. By making money free speech, the courts increased the free flow of money and access to politicians. This also makes our country great because who better to tell politicians what to do than corporations that create all these jobs we have.

With the courts on our side, we finally got rid of illogical anti-corporate laws that restricted what we could do with our money to influence government. Now we can buy other corporations, influence politics, write our own laws, and pretty near have our own way. Laws and decisions giving corporations rights in the 1970s secured much of the great influence and power we have today. Letting corporations rule keeps this country on top.

Corporate Criminals: Liberals Trying to Stop us from Helping America

There's a dark cloud over this happy fairytale ending for corporations: corporate criminals. These corporate criminals are being called out in this chapter to stand in line and be accountable, to face the music and pay the piper while reaping what they sow. These criminals are vicious and include the following groups:

- Lawyers who want to sue corporations out of existence.
- Ralph Nader who wants to make corporations responsible for everything that goes wrong in people's lives.
- Eco-terrorists and environmentalists who think spotted owls, the Colorado River, and a few old growth trees are more important than profit making corporations. Note the word environ**mental**ist has the word "mental" in it. That proves we should ignore them.
- Democrats, who want to "regulate" us.
- Scientists, who think that a few hundred studies prove our products like tobacco, do harm.
- Anti-globalization forces that are simply nut jobs, as Thomas Friedman has proven in his book <u>The World is Flat</u>. They just don't want to face reality. You see, the world is flat, and science just lies that it's round.
- Unions, who think workers deserve a living wage
- Human rights kooks, who think we should help workers in Saipan who make ten pairs of shoes for two dollars a day for shoes we sell for only $120.
- Jealous loser-liberals, who dislike Starbucks and Wal-Mart because they sell things and are successful.

Tort Reform and Drug Protections

There are lawyers out there trying to ruin America and make money through unnecessary lawsuits against innocent corporations. That is why we need tort reform.

Tort reform is something corporations came up with because they needed a reason to stop liability lawsuits against them. If we can get enough people to see that lawyers are out of control and trying to harm hardworking corporations through lawsuits, we can put an end to corporate responsibility.

Just because corporations create things like cigarettes, asbestos, lead toys, pollution, and drugs that harm people, it doesn't mean people should be able to sue them. Tort reform is a good idea because it protects corporations from having to pay for things they do that accidentally hurt people. We all make mistakes, don't we? Why should we let these liberal whiners throw the first stones? Liberal lawyers, a redundancy, tell us that lawsuits only get to trial if there's really something to it. Well, I protest your honor. Sustained!!

Conservative folks like me know that lawsuits are out of control, and we can come up with a lawsuit or two that sounds ridiculous to back us up. Finding one case, just *one case* that is out of control, confirms that *all* lawsuits that hurt our profit are frivolous. After that, we can talk on and on about how *all* lawsuits are frivolous. One bad apple spoils the whole barrel. The woman who sued McDonalds for giving her coffee that was too hot (she'd probably sue if it was too cold) proves that frivolous lawsuits exist. Frivolous lawsuits also exist because I say so.

What we patriots of the Right won't tell you about are all the fail-safes that are in the legal code to prevent frivolous lawsuits. That is just liberal hogwash they use to confuse us. They tell us that ambulance-chasing lawyers don't exist. I know for a fact that they do because I watch television and have seen those ads for the "accident" lawyers.

Well sure, lawyers in civil cases work on contingency, meaning they don't get paid for lawyering unless they win the lawsuit. Lawyers may be liberal and corrupt, but they're so greedy that they would never take on a lawsuit they couldn't win.

Some liberals say it's because the lawsuits are not frivolous. However, lawyers have the skills to make any lawsuit seem real with their golden tongues and lying skills. Judges, being stupid and corrupt, are easily fooled by such lawyering into thinking that any lawsuit has merit. Even though they work for free if a case doesn't pay off, the lawsuits against any corporation, no matter the specifics of the case, are still frivolous.

Another part of the system that us Billionaires and friends of Bush fail to tell you about is that if a plaintiff, the person suing the corporation, fails to show cause and can't bring a real case against the company, the plaintiff can be made liable for the legal fees paid by the defendant, the innocent and victimized company. This is called "summary judgment", and this legal payback has been in place since 1937. We fail to broadcast information about this summary judgment in our media; it might cause some people to lose interest in tort reform.

Let's imagine that not all judges are corrupt and stupid. If they aren't all corrupt and stupid, and they know that their bread is buttered by Republicans who put them in office, they will work to reduce or eliminate judgments against our corporations. That's how we get direct verdicts against our corporations stopped, reduced, or deemed illegal.

If a judge isn't wise enough to cut the compensation given by juries, there are a series of appeals that corporations can use to block judgments for years. And if it's a judgment in favor of a plaintiff who is really sick due to corporate liability (which doesn't exist, it's all *consumer responsibility)*, the plaintiff might die before they get their money. Judges can also reduce the jury award, as they did in the famous McDonalds case. The jury awarded $2.7 million to the coffee scalded woman, but the judge cut that to $480,000.

The American Tort Reform Association (ATRA) has been working hard on changing the law to make lawyers more reasonable when bringing suits against corporations. The ATRA wants to reduce the number of liability lawsuits even though the Seventh Amendment tells us that we can sue people (and corporations *are* people) and have a jury in a civil case. Backed by Karl Rove, who likes to take money away from the Democrat loving liberal lawyerism, the ATRA studied some 3,141 lawsuits in 2004 looking for frivolous suits.

What they found, shockingly, were an outrageous *two* abuses of judicial torts out of the 3,141 they investigated (Zegart). As you know by now, we only need *one* bad lawsuit as an example to show all lawsuits are bad. We got twice as many as we needed, so we can plow ahead because about .06% of all corporate liability lawsuits are frivolous. In addition, corporate lawyers can appeal those three out of five thousand lawsuits when the courts make mistakes.

Then there is the case of legal harassment against Wal-Mart. States are trying to sue Wal-Mart for not paying employees what they promised and not giving lazy Wal-Mart workers the lunch breaks state laws require. Thankfully, out of the hundreds of suits against Wal-Mart, only four class action suits were brought against them for this so-called employee abuse. Although this worker abuse is a nationwide problem, the federal courts saw the lawsuits for what they were. It is corporate bashing by a bunch of whiny employees. Therefore, judges didn't allow lawyers to take most of these cases to the federal bench for a class action suit.

Good Medicine

Tort reform is good for tobacco and asbestos manufacturers, but those products are going out of style. Pharmaceutical companies are working hard to get everyone taking drugs for something. If you're not using drugs yet, you're in denial. Because of the demand for drugs, drug companies don't always have time to get the drugs tested the way they would like. In several years, there may be millions of people that want to sue drug companies. With tort reform, those innocent drug-dealing companies won't need to worry about vicious citizens suing. That would be true even if the drugs these companies manufactured, at huge profits, made their customers sick.

Tort reform will cut out the state lawsuits for FDA approved medication and only allow federal suits. Since the federal judges are more conservative, chosen by our man Bush, and like to cut damage awards, the current drug company profits will more than cover any future lawsuits. Thank God for tort reform.

NAFTA or Bust

Thomas Friedman is a writer for the liberal New York Times. Thomas Friedman supports free trade. Therefore, all liberals support free trade. Because conservatives also support free trade, it proves that free trade is good for America and the world.

Free trade has been the mantra of modern economists since the Chicago school of economics and Milton Friedman said it was the best way to make money. Free trade means that there will be no barriers to the trade of goods and services between countries. There will also be no tariffs or quotas placed upon goods going from one country to another.

Free Trade is Patriotic

People who don't like free trade despise America. They're stupid and they don't live in reality, *our* reality. No matter what you read, hear or see, people against globalization are all traitors. There's no need to read or listen to anything these traitors have to say because it will just be more treason and therefore support terrorists. In fact, you hate America for just listening or reading a point of view other than ours. If you have betrayed America with free speech, the only way to redeem yourself is to listen to and believe everything I say. Take that Al Franken!

Like corporations, free trade helped the Colonists beat the British in the Revolutionary War. It makes this country great. Free trade has been instrumental in helping America in many ways.

- Free trade allowed labor to move freely from Africa to the United States before the civil war. Liberals call these workers "slaves".
- Free trade demanded that we defend bananas in Guatemala in 1954 when we invaded Guatemala to save the United Fruit Company.

- Free trade helped us defend democracy in Chile and Argentina when it was threatened in the 1970s and 80s. There's more about that in chapter VI.
- Free trade has allowed American corporations to utilize a world pool of labor, helping workers everywhere.
- Corporations made American democracy possible; therefore, opening countries to free trade will make all countries more democratic. Just look at the great democracies of Nigeria, Saudi Arabia, China, and Indonesia if you need examples of how free trade helps democratization.
- Free trade has eliminated the drudgery of farm work for millions of people worldwide. This dislodged them from their land and introduced them to the wonders of industrial labor.
- Free trade creates elites who are willing to use extreme measures to keep their population down in order to stop them from hassling us all over the world.
- Free trade keeps unions down at home and abroad, and as we know because I said it, unions are satanic, communist, and un-American!

NAFTA (the North American Free Trade Agreement) was passed over the objections of much of America and went into full effect in January 1994. How did it pass? Fear. The United States government said that if we didn't get free trade now, we were going to lose out and communism would prevail. Who fought against NAFTA? Unions, environmentalists, human rights workers, animal rights organizations, and other liberals, that's who. Surprisingly, many Democrats such as Al Gore, Bill Clinton, John Kerry, and Nancy Pelosi supported NAFTA. Even these traitors couldn't stand up against the rightness of free trade.

NAFTA helps workers in the United States, Canada, and Mexico. Here's the story (the truths we spout) most U.S. economists tell the people about NAFTA.

NAFTA has increased Mexican exports. Thankfully, it's the rich corporations that control exports in Mexico. However, the exports are from U.S. companies with *maquiladoras* (Mexican factories on the border) in Mexico. Exports have increased and the profits have gone to the richest, most worthy people.

National income has gone up in Mexico since NAFTA. That's all you need to know because we want to tell you how it helps workers and average citizens. The whole country is richer, but real wages for average workers are down in Mexico since NAFTA. That makes Mexico great.

One in five people in Mexico is employed in export jobs, and that's not counting drug and human smugglers (mules and coyotes). Even if Mexicans aren't over here cleaning up my yard, they're still working to make me consumer goods.

Farm production is up under NAFTA. Over a million people will have had to leave their land in Mexico to work in maquiladoras or cross the border to look for work in the United States. Large industrial farms are more productive than all those small farms, so people have to move to the border, or go over the border, to look for work (O'Neil, et al).

The point is the "big picture", meaning macroeconomics, is what's important. There is no reason to look at what's happening for the individual. NAFTA made things so much better in Mexico; therefore, more people are crossing the border into the United States than ever before (ibid). Macroeconomics tells us that if economic indicators are up for large corporations, everyone is doing better. That is what we tell people, so they don't get worried.

How to use Economic Statistics

There are good statistics and there are bad statistics. That means that there's what we want you to believe, and what you see is happening to you. Good statistics show what a great, powerful, and rich country we are. Good statistics are patriotic and play in the mass media.

Good statistics support the economic policies of the right wing and the economic enrichment of the top 1% so we can help the lower classes later. Good statistics allow us to use facts to spin the economy for a public that just doesn't understand how good they have it. The good statistics show how well corporations are running things.

Bad statistics are unpatriotic and should be ignored. When the media mentions a bad economic fact, it gives aid and comfort to the terrorists. Bad statistics are for poor people who want excuses for not pulling themselves up by their own bootstraps. Why I mention them is beyond me.

Good Statistics

The stock market is growing—we know that as the stock market goes up, everyone gets richer. Moreover, *everyone* owns lots of stocks. This is a good statistic unless the stock market goes down. In that case, we should ignore it.

GNP—Gross national product means the total value of goods and services that all us U.S. citizens produce in the United States or overseas, and it's almost always going up! That means all those companies that incorporate overseas to avoid taxes count as part of the GNP. This makes GNP a good statistic. Rich folks are getting richer, and that raises the GNP. However, it doesn't mean we should be forced to share our wealth. We also love GNP because it plays in the media and shows the people that everything is okay.

The "official" unemployment rate.—We like that because it legitimizes all sorts of conservative policies, from free trade to welfare reform. Once people were counted when they didn't have a job. With the new welfare reform started under Clinton, you don't count as unemployed when you stop looking for work and stop collecting unemployment insurance. So that unemployment rate is really the rate of those receiving unemployment compensation.

Only those who get laid off, and only those who were laid off recently, will be counted in this statistic. It underreports unemployment and makes the economy look better than it really is. That keeps consumer confidence up, and keeps us in tall cotton.

CEO earnings—because CEOs are so important, it's good to see their wages going up. This means that the companies they run are doing better and there's more employment. Executive pay jumped 571 percent between 1990 and 2000 (Institute for Policy Studies). That's good news for everyone because before 1990, CEOs were underpaid. They only made single digit millions at the time. CEOs earn their salaries.

- They send jobs overseas; it's tough work laying-off thousands.
- They create more Billionaires. That way, I can have more yacht club buddies.
- They save taxes for corporations and raise fees on the poor instead of giving them handouts.
- CEOs successfully lobby Congress and get our candidates elected. Then, we get to help them with the burden of re-writing the tax code.
- They reduce inflation by keeping wages low.
- They help cut social welfare so they can donate to charities and look noble.

Business investment—hey, it's going up, so that proves things are going well for everyone!

Exports—because there are more exports, there is more wealth for everyone.

Productivity—this means we're squeezing more value out of each employee and replacing more of them with more machines so each one of them that we actually pay is making more value for the people for whom they work.

Bad Statistics

Poverty rate—it tells us that poverty has been increasing in the United States since Bush was elected. Nevertheless, I proved poverty doesn't exist in chapter three. Yes, the poverty rate records something that doesn't exist, or something that is your fault anyway, so why should we count it?

Hunger—again, if people weren't lazy, they would be working and wouldn't be hungry. We shouldn't look at this statistic because it doesn't look at the amount of food wasted in the United States that if people had the gumption, they could collect and eat from the dumpsters.

Real wages (wage increases minus inflation) are stagnant or going down for most since 1980—what's this mumbo jumbo about wages going down anyway? Wages are really going up, and to include the cost of living (a rise in inflation) to show that what we really earn is going down is just a bunch of cow pies. People have more money. What do price increases have to do with it?

Uninsured—so what if forty-eight million Americans don't have health insurance? What does that have to do with the economy anyway? Liberals are always trying to find a way to lie about the economy, and linking people's health to the economic health of a nation is just another example. English, French, and Ottoman economies did quite well during the black plague in the fourteenth century, so that proves there is no link between health and economics.

Income gap—liberals talk about how CEOs and other management are making so much more than the average worker makes. Depending on what liberal stats you read, CEOs make 250 to 300 times what an average worker makes (ibid). So what! I've already proven earlier that CEOs earned it.

Stop the "Death" Tax; Make Death Less Taxing

There's this thing liberals call the "estate tax". These are taxes liberals want to put on rich families that earned their money fair and square. How dare they try to tax multimillionaires on 20% of the income that they pass down to their children. So what if the first $7 million of inheritance isn't taxed? It should be completely eliminated.

What we über-rich know is that the death tax will hurt family businesses. People won't want to pass their businesses on to their children and pay all that tax. The estate tax will also hurt family farms because family farms are so popular. Family farms are all going out of business because of taxes and not because of cutthroat competition from mega farms and agribusinesses.

Not only will the estate tax will hurt families, it will hurt women and minorities. Because many women and minorities run small and medium size businesses, it will hurt them. Thus, workers will get laid off when these medium and small businesses fail due to the death tax.

Furthermore, low-income people will get hurt because this tax encourages spending, according to William Beach of the Heritage Foundation (Adopted from Beach 2).

If you believe all of this, I salute you. I salute you because you believe exactly what the great Walton family of Wal-Mart and Sam's Club fame wants you to believe. Even though the tax only gets paid by the richest 2% of all families who have members die, it will hurt the other 98% of you who don't have to worry about being taxed at all when you die. Furthermore, the first seven million dollars of the top 2% won't be taxed at all, but we ALL should be concerned about the estate tax anyway. I will be cryogenically preserved so I never die and have to pay this evil tax. I suggest you do that too.

Liberals tell us that family farms don't generally pass the seven million dollar threshold and don't pay estate taxes. How do they know? Liberals are way to lazy to own a family farm, or look up tax records to find out that there are so few family farms left.

Women and minorities, liberals all, have businesses that are small or medium and aren't wealthy enough to pay an estate tax. Whose fault is it that they don't have good enough business sense to be worth more than seven million dollars. Women and minority owned businesses would be hurt if they owned more than seven million dollars of assets and didn't have the tax shelters to protect their money.

Workers will get hurt by the estate tax, you'll see. When a Walton family member dies and pays his estate tax, the Wal-Mart workers will get laid off, of course. Liberals think the Waltons are so super rich that they can afford to pay something back to the government that has kept taxes low for them for so long. That's liberal thinking for you.

What liberals don't understand is that one reason the Waltons got so rich is that they are Republicans and don't use bad liberal accounting practices like giving money away to unnecessary taxes. I salute William Beach for pointing out how this death tax will hurt us all. As you see, the death tax hurts so many people because rich people who have to pay it. Billionaires won't be able to afford that extra yacht or jet they've been eying. That will hurt everyone.

Special Rules for Special People

Now you realize how great corporations have been for everyone. Therefore, corporations should live by an enhanced set of rules. Because of their economic power, corporations can buy political power. Corporations have more money, so they are more worthy. That is the bottom line in God's design.

While individuals can donate to political campaigns at thousand dollars a shot, which most of you can't afford, corporate leaders can easily bundle $100,000 together, start a political action committee (PAC), buy ads that support candidates' positions and send politicians on "junkets", those special trips that "don't influence the way Congress votes" to quote many a politician. The rules that work for corporations in the corporate age include no-bid contracts and special accounting practices. Let's start with no-bid contracts.

No Need for a Resume

One of the greatest things we received from this White House is the no-bid contract. The government knows that they don't have the time to take bids if they're in the midst of a crisis, and no-bid contracts are needed for national security. A no-bid contract is like your daddy giving you a fat check and the keys to the safe without you having to apply for the job. The cronies of Bush and Cheney are treated like family and given the contracts they need to survive. Liberals think we can just sit around and compare bids when there's an ongoing war. However, comparing numbers is hard, time-consuming work.

When we create a crisis, we don't have to take any bids. If there's a war or hurricane, the government can just hire a corporation to do cleanup or supply security. You wouldn't ask for a resume from a relative or friend if they offered to help you clean the garage or fix the fence, so why would we ask our corporate relatives and friends for bids to do work for us? Competition for contracts would damage national security. Why bid for jobs in Iraq, New Orleans, Afghanistan, and airports and for military and security contracts when the President has so many friends in business that are willing to do the work.

According to Michael Dobbs of that liberal Washington Post, Halliburton, which used to be headed by Vice President Cheney, got contracts worth more than $1.7 billion to go into Iraq to rebuild it. They made hundreds of millions more dollars under no-bid contracts given to them by the U.S. Army (Dobbs). Dobbs writes that corporations run operations that cost one-third of the monthly costs of maintaining troops in Iraq, about $1 billion a month. Only $1 billion a month for support services? That is quite a sacrifice.

Companies involved in Iraq range from small consulting firms run by retired generals to big traditional corporations that rent out commandos. There are a lot of these firms (a hundred or so), and they work all over the world helping democracy and earning over $100 billion a year (ibid).

One of these companies is the consulting firm Blackwater, and they do everything they do to help their workers despite evidence to the contrary. Some crazy families want to sue Blackwater because they didn't properly armor their vehicles Iraq, and some Blackwater mercenaries were killed. Talk about your frivolous lawsuit! Didn't these workers know they might get killed in Iraq? They do use real bullets.

They didn't have the full number of people per vehicle for protective fire (three instead of four) so they couldn't defend from rear attacks. Blackwater was just trying to save the United States people money on unnecessary employment of security personnel. People didn't die because they didn't have the right amount of support. They died because those Iraqis are tricky, and they're crack shots.

Blackwater is also being accused of shooting people that they weren't supposed to. It is a war zone. Don't people have the right to shoot? The Blackwater workers were just recognizing that all Arabs are terrorists and shot the Iraqis preemptively.

Accounting Practices that work: CEOs Changing Dates

Imagine you bought a $200,000 house in the year 2000. However, you don't pay up front, you pay when you sell the house. Then you want to sell the house in the year 2005 for $250,000, but you really want to make more money. What to do? You date the purchase of your house back to say, 1975, when it was worth $100,000. By paying only $100,000 on a house worth $200,000 when you actually bought it, you get an extra $100,000. That's what CEOs and other corporate executives do when they are offered stock options because in essence, they don't really own it or pay for it; they get the money if they sell the stock at a profit.

By backdating the stock offer to a time when the stock was lower, it creates the biggest possible gain when selling the stock. They dated the stock options to a time when the stock was low so they could make say, an extra million dollars on 100,000 shares. They took advantage and made money that they would invest back in our economy on things such as Bentleys and gold plated golf clubs that keep Americans employed.

UnitedHealth Group Chairman and CEO William McGuire got very flexible options. He could pick whatever date he wanted in order to back date stocks to the lowest point and thus take greatest advantage of stock price increases. He got help from their board of directors who also got in on the deal.

Some liberals don't like this practice because they think it rips off stockholders who can't backdate their stock purchases, and that it puts regular people at an unfair disadvantage. However, it doesn't hurt anyone if the execs make a little more money. What's the big deal? So what if heads of Fortune 500 companies (at least forty are being investigated for backdating, probably more) might lose interest in keeping their company profitable if they can cash out whenever they want. They wouldn't do anything that was actually illegal.

Here are some of the companies under persecutorial investigation by the SEC, other regulators, or grand juries as reported by the companies themselves: UnitedHealth Group, Brooks Automation, F5 Networks, Openwave Systems, Sycamore Networks, RSA Security, SafeNet, Semtech, Comverse Technology, Juniper Networks, KLA-Tencor, Vitesse Semiconductor, and NYFIX (Bush). I don't see what the big deal is. These multimillionaires are manipulating stock to make millions while granny and everyone else is loosing their pensions. Become a CEO if you want to do the hard work of making millions off the labor of others.

Abramoff: A crisis we like

We like the Abramoff crisis. Our former ally, Jack Abramoff, got caught stealing from Indian Tribes (about sixty-six million dollars) and for paying for access to Abramoff's friend at that time, speaker of the house, Tom Delay. There are those "bad elements" in the lobbying world, we weeded them out, and the system works. Bush had many contacts with Abramoff who, while not stealing from Indians, was lobbying for Republicans and charging millions because of his White House and Congressional connections.

You might think it looks bad for Bush. Not at all. Bush can't control rogue lobbyists! The Abramoff crisis helps us hide the regular practice of campaign donations influencing how Congress votes for laws and how corporations like drug companies help Congress write the laws.

Jack Abramoff knew how to work the system. Through a front group called *The United States Family Network* (USFN), Abramoff was able to get Alabama residents (mostly the avowed Christians) to block Indian Gambling and a lottery in the state. The trickery was that Abramoff's real clients were Choctaw Indians that already had a casino in nearby Philadelphia, Mississippi. They had hired "Casino Jack" to block the new application for a casino in Alabama using a state referendum. Casinos can't abide nearby competition from other casinos or state lotteries.

Once again, we see right wing consultants, heroes of the little guy, using "Christian values" to get things done. In this case, gambling rights of the Choctaws were protected. By the way, Abramoff got paid $82 million from Indian tribes who run casinos. So, he does right, and gets paid (Anniston Star).

Who else did Uncle "Casino Jack" help? Russian oil interest *Naftasib* (so clever of them to put the word "NAFTA" in their name). Abramoff knows Tom Delay, and Tom Delay was the speaker of the house when *Naftasib*

Corporations Should Run Everything

needed help to keep its stock afloat in Russia. The problem was that the Russian economy was in the tank and needed International Monetary Fund (IMF) loans to stay afloat. If Russia didn't get the loans, Russian oil *Naftasib* would go under.

Nevskaya and Alexander Koulakovsky of Naftasib gave $1 million dollars to a London Law firm, which in turn gave the money to the United States Family Network who gave the money to Republican campaigns, including Tom Delay. Then Delay, who had dinner in Moscow with the Koulakovskys and also got money from Abramoff's casino clients, helped secure the IMF loans to help out the Russians. Therefore, one hand washes the other, and they all come away clean. The graph explains how the influence peddling worked.

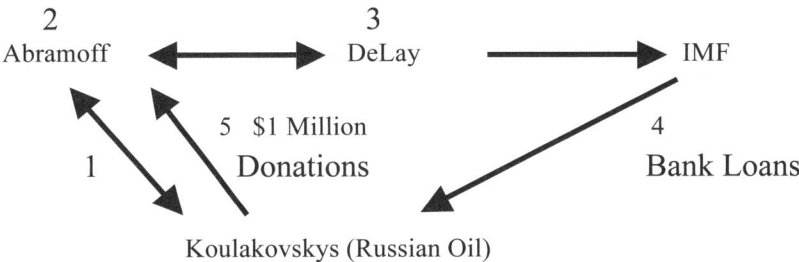

There is nothing wrong with all of this influence peddling. However, Delay did get indicted and had to leave his House seat, and Abramoff went off to jail. This all happened because Abramoff was trying to help the good gambling companies and Russian oil firms. If corporations were in charge, this would never have happened because payola wouldn't be a crime. Pay to play would be the rule. While it still is very popular, we'd like you to think of this case as *thee* exception. Buying influence in Washington, D.C. never happens.

Thank you, Jack Abramoff, for helping with one of the biggest stories that keep us in power; there is no payback for giving money to political campaigns. Jack Abramoff helped funnel donations to USFN and to political campaigns. As Abramoff said, "I just don't think members of Congress for the most part sell their votes ... generally speaking, that is (ibid)." Generally speaking. However, Abramoff plead guilty in January 2006 to fraud, tax evasion, and conspiracy to channel gifts, trips, and campaign contributions to members of Congress.

Abramoff also gave trips, meals, money, entertainment, and other perks to help Congress decide how to vote. Rob Ney, Congressman from Ohio, got caught taking a trip to Scotland that Abramoff paid for to get Ney's support for laws his clients backed. But, there is NO proof that these trips guaranteed votes. Other people (remember, corporations ARE people) get to call Congress and send letters to their representatives. It is only fair that corporations, who are legally individuals, can send Congress gifts as well.

Protecting Pharmaceutical Rights

Some patients want to take away the rights of pharmaceutical companies just because people are sick and need help. Thankfully, the estimated $400 billion dollar *Medicaid Overhaul Bill* passed in 2003. We know government messes everything up, so the new Medicare program will rely on private insurance for the delivery of drug benefits. Not only that, it shares the drug development and advertising costs with you, the taxpayer.

The prices of prescription drugs have been going up like a quail in hunting season. The more sick people there are, the more the companies can charge them. That's the law of supply and demand. Drug companies can rake in millions trying to make people feel healthy after food and energy companies get people sick with growth hormones and pollution.

The drug bill protects the pharmaceutical companies. The government won't be able to negotiate drug prices under the new Medicare bill, though Democrats are trying to change that. Large companies and government agencies can get discounts on drug prices when buying in bulk, and they pass the savings on to employees. Prescription drugs are too important for national security to float on the free market for Medicare recipients.

The consumer pays a little more to preserve democracy. Drug companies aren't working for free you know. The Veterans Administration gets discounts for drugs going to veterans by buying in bulk. But you don't think seniors and the disabled deserve the same discounts veterans get, do you? If you do, you love Osama Bin Laden (Nader).

Another great thing is that this bill doesn't interfere with the market prices of drugs, so it doesn't do anything communist like control the rising cost of prescriptions or the huge profits drug companies make. The $720 billion cost for the law ends up in the pockets of the beleaguered drug companies that keep America strong. Some say the bill might cost up to 1.2 trillion (Connolly and Allen A01). As we know, the only way a medical plan can run is if drug and insurance companies make huge profits. The more profit they make, the better off America is.

Medicare drug reform also gets people off traditional Medicare and into the managed health coverage. You have to leave traditional Medicare coverage to get the prescription drug benefit; you get a voucher to pay private insurance companies for care. Then the market takes over. There is no further guarantee of coverage and you lose the government guarantee of care under the old Medicare. Hardly any limits will be put on company premiums and deductibles (costs for services that insurance companies tell you they cover). Therefore, the Medicare bill is good for America and good for democracy because it's good for business.

Once under the new Medicare drug plan, seniors won't be able to buy supplemental coverage for cost overruns on medical treatment. This is yet another example how we love the free market that we control. This captive group of consumers will keep the companies and the program strong and help everyone. With the help of pharmaceutical and insurance companies, the medical system in the United States works and stays safe from socialized medicine. That is why we should let corporations run our health care (Park, et al).

Corporations Should Run Education

I have a private education and that's what made me so smart and rich. I did not, as liberals suggest, get a head start with my Papa Shelters who made it rich on offshore oil and inshore prison labor. I earned the jobs he gave me and chose to be born into a good family, thus proving my superiority.

The only people that defend public education are teachers, parents, administrators, unions, public service employees, advocates for the poor, wacko journalists, social workers, people who can't afford private education, some Democrats, hippies, and a few misguided liberal Republicans. They're all liberal nutcases who know nothing about education and don't know a bad thing when they see one.

Bush had it right with *No Child Left Behind*. He let corporations in on the deal to make it even better because corporations, as we all know, put children before profits. All you have to do is go to visit Indonesian or Thai factories run by benevolent corporations that allow ten-year-old boys and girls work to keep their families from starving to know how much corporations care.

No Child Left Behind (NCLB) is helping America in so many ways. It makes schools accountable by increasing the testing requirements at schools and forcing schools to test students and flunk students if they don't pass the test. And if lots of students flunk at a school, the schools flunk. Then we can stop wasting our money on these loser schools. In fact, 95% of the students need to be tested and 80% need to pass for the schools to get a passing grade (Bracey).

Accountability is just one aspect of NCLB and it helps to get the American people to support NCLB. Another good thing about this law is that it makes publishing corporations millions of dollars. States will spend billions for the required tests, according to the non-partisan Government Accounting Office (ibid). So, instead of throwing money at the problem schools to buy books, fix leaky roofs, unclog the plumbing, patch holes in the walls, secure faulty structures, and hire teachers to reduce classroom sizes from fifty to say a manageable thirty (Kozol), we test these precious little future consumers. The government understands that what we really need to improve the schools is making them liable for more testing.

This testing is promoted and created by the White House and corporate leaders from major publishing companies. CEOs understand how to use education to make better, more compliant workers. Education should not be allowed to fail in meeting the standards corporations set. If students don't become good corporate citizens, they will become outcasts and might be tempted by the lure of liberals or gays. The people who worked on this bill include heads of Fortune 500 companies such as Harold McGraw, chairman of McGraw-Hill, who feels that education is benefited by a sublimation of the public and the education community to business and political leaders (Bracey).

The bill gave $387 million to states to start testing, but The National Association of State Boards of Education says it could cost anywhere from $2.7 billion to $7 billion (Metcalf). This money could be spent in states to improve the schools in other ways than testing, but if we don't stop these liberal schools by bankrupting them, how else can we do it?

This law has other benefits. The testing helps the publishing companies and hires more Americans. It also puts liberal teachers on notice to get with the corporate model of education or get fired. With all the time teachers spend on testing, and preparing for the test, they'll have less time to brainwash the students by educating them.

NCLB was possible because the Bush family knew they could rely on the McGraw family to sell their testing to Congress. The McGraws and Bushes have known each other for about seventy years. Harold McGraw III helped President Bush's transition into the White House as part of his team along with McGraw-Hill board member Edward Rust Jr. Because of this relationship, McGraw-Hill publishing was willing to sell the NCLB testing materials to the Bush government (ibid).

McGraw-Hill did the research that made it possible for Bush to use their testing materials. The company sold books to the Texas Department of Education when President Bush was the governor there. Without this close relationship between the makers of the NCLB tests and the White House, this great law might never have happened and those billions of dollars might have been wasted on public schools instead of tests.

This benefits everyone; it allows publishers to stay on top against fierce competition from foreign testing companies and stay ahead of the testing gap. The idea that we need testing, and we *have* to get Bush's friends to sell the tests, keeps America great. Yet again, we realize that corporations should run everything.

Corporations and War: A Winning Team

Corporations have helped the United States win every war in its history. They have sacrificed their hard earned capital to help the United States procure the weapons of war. In fact, U.S. corporations have often decided what countries to attack. Without this corporate help, peace might break out, and the U.S. would be crippled.

You need manpower such as soldiers, service staff, medical personnel, drivers, and politicians to send off the troops to win a war. You also need guns, tanks, planes, ships, bombs and other weapons. Then there are the uniforms, the beds, the helmets, the buildings and other things. War infrastructure is a winning industry in this country. As long as the United States is making people in the world angry, there is nothing to stop our military build-up.

Military-Industrial-Congressional Complex

Since the country began, the United States has had an alliance between the leaders of corporations and Congress. Corporations would provide much needed weapons to Congress, and Congress would provide contracts for corporations. Look at how corporations supported World War I (chapter I, pg 21) and you'll see that huge war profits are the price of freedom, because "freedom isn't free".

Why do the liberals complain that we don't like to create jobs? Continued *war*ateering has worked so well that weapons are one of our number biggest exports in dollar value. A report by the Congressional Research Service found that the monetary value of U.S. arms exports in 2004 exceeded $18 billion (Boese). The United States is making a killing in weapons exports. According to the recently released Small Arms Survey, the United States exports more small arms and light weapons than any other country - four times as many as its closest competitor, Germany. Let the Germans have their VWs and BMWs and the French have their wine and foreign films, we are the tops in arms sales. It makes you proud to be American. Many jobs would be lost if peace were to break out.

Weapon Systems We Need, Because I Say so

Liberals say we should cut down on military spending because they are weak on terrorism. We need a big military budget because it seems the more countries we liberate overseas, Iraq and Afghanistan just being the most recent, the more people want to hurt us. Call it envy or meanness, but we need to stay strong. In addition, our military budget is only as large as all other military budgets in the world. Our military budget should be three times as large as the rest of the world.

We need to build more F-22 attack planes. We wanted the F-22 because it would be better than anything the Soviet Union had, and they only cost $150 million per plane. We only have more F-15s and F-16s then any other military has of their attack planes. And our planes are much better than their planes. We must constantly be concerned and in fear that we fall behind; therefore, we must build more and more weaponry. Everyone is out to get us because they envy our freedoms.

Liberals say there is fraud and waste in military spending. This kind of talk supports our enemies and terrorists. By letting terrorists know we're wasting money on our military, it makes us vulnerable to terrorism. For example, liberals want to cut the Osprey Attack helicopter plane because it does the exact thing that our planes and helicopters already do, but not as well. Each plane was to cost $96.2 million, then $114.8 million per aircraft, and recently $159.7 million per aircraft. These Osprey Attack helicopters also fail at a high rate. That means Boeing and Bell get to build more and make more money, and we need more money.

Each branch of the military needs their own attack plane. They can't share, and that means more money for us. There's the Air Force's F-22 Raptor (Lockheed Martin, Boeing, and the Pratt and Whitney Division of United Technologies, $5.2 billion program). It's still the best, and costs the most! Then there is the Navy's F-18E/F fighter plane (Boeing, General Electric, and Northrop Grumman, $3.3 billion program). It's also expensive, so we still build them. Then the Air Force has its Joint Strike Fighter/F-35 (Lockheed Martin and Northrop Grumman, $3.5 billion program). Watch out terrorists!

The Navy gets their own goodies with the Virginia class attack submarine (Electric Boat Division of General Dynamics and the Newport News Shipbuilding division of Northrop Grumman, at only $2.3 billion per submarine. It's a bargain. Then there's the Trident II Submarine-Launched Ballistic Missile (Lockheed Martin Missiles and Space, $626 million: unit Cost: $30.9 million). We need these missiles because we need to be able to shoot nukes from submarines at sea and not just by land (Hartung).

This is just an example of how well we spend our money. The current budget is more of the same with an estimated $504,863,000,000 dollars for defense in 2007 (United States Department of Defense). That is up from $474 billion in 2005. Money for defense is easy to get. The liberals keep asking for more money for wasteful projects like education, levee reinforcement, vaccinations, water purification, police departments, health care, and so forth. We will not be coerced into helping the public when our nation is at risk. We must stay strong.

Persecuted Corporations

The scientists at the *Bulletin of the Atomic Scientists* persecute weapons contractors by telling us that one out of ten contractors have been convicted of, or admitted to, defrauding the government between 1980 and 1992. They make up facts to hurt people because they're scientists and they're liberal. What follows is a list of some of the corporations liberals are persecuting.

- Defense contractor Grumman paid the government $20 million to escape criminal liability for coercing subcontractors into making political contributions. In fact, they were just very persuasive.
- Lockheed was convicted of paying millions in bribes to obtain classified planning documents. They were just trying to get an honest jump up on the competition.
- Northrop was fined $17 million for falsifying test data on its cruise missiles and fighter jets. Just because some secretary made a mistake on a report, didn't mean they were guilty of anything.
- Rockwell was fined $5.5 million for committing criminal fraud against the Air Force.
- Boeing, Grumman, Hughes, Raytheon and RCA pleaded guilty to illegal trafficking in classified documents and paid a total of almost $15 million in restitution, reimbursements, fines, etc. How were they to know those F-22 plans were classified?
- Hughes pleaded guilty to procurement fraud in one case, was convicted of it in a second case and, along with McDonnell Douglas and General Motors, settled out-of-court for a total of more than $1 million dollars in a third case.
- Teledyne, a defense electronics firm, paid $5 million in a civil settlement for false testing, plus $5 million for repairs. Again with the persecution! Why didn't the government let corporations comply with their own test-

ing? I mean, who better to know if their systems are working then the defense contractors?

- McDonnell Douglas settled for a total of more than $22 million in four "defective pricing" cases.

General Electric was the most persecuted contractor. They were convicted for mail and procurement fraud that resulted in a criminal fine of $10 million and restitution of $2.2 million. GE was also forced to plead guilty in 1961 for price-fixing and paid a $372,500 fine. In 1977, the government entrapped GE for price-fixing again. In 1979, they were framed and forced to settle out-of-court by the State of Alabama for allegedly dumping PCBs in a river. In 1981, it was again set up by the government and for allegedly bribing Puerto Rican officials. GE was coerced to plead guilty in 1985 on 108 counts of fraud on a Minuteman missile contract. In addition, an engineer at GE was convicted of perjury, and GE paid a fine of a million dollars to avoid further persecution and witch hunting by the jack booted lawyers in the Justice Department.

In 1985, GE pleaded guilty to falsifying time cards. They only did this to protect a few corrupt workers who were dealt with later. In 1989, GE again paid the government $3.5 million in a protection racket scheme to settle five civil lawsuits alleging contractor fraud at a jet-engine plant the government said they were over billing. In 1990, the usually honest army lied about criminal fraud accusing the perpetually honest GE of cheating the Army on a contract for battlefield computers (Zepezauer 1996).

Just like Christians, corporations are blamed for everything that goes wrong in America. The bureaucrats at the Justice Department don't know how hard corporations work to please the demanding and domineering slave drivers at the Pentagon. Just like investment in R&D for the pharmaceutical companies should allow drug makers to charge whatever they want for drugs, cost overruns are a natural part of the business of creating military weapons and those cost overruns should be allowed and passed on to consumers.

Corporate Democracy for Everyone

Corporations started slowly in this nation. Eventually, we learned to use our money to our advantage. We got laws passed for us, can now hold our charters for life, and we are legally seen as people. As people, we can invest in politicians that give us the tax cuts we need. How else could we send jobs overseas and get a tax cut to do so. We can shelter our profits by incorporating overseas, and we will soon be able to skirt corporate liability lawsuits. All this was because we have sold the idea that without us, you'd be a pig without slop. We are now creating a democracy of the corporations, for the corporations, and by the corporations. We have created so much democracy, that "Democracy is Our Number One Export".

Chapter VI

Democracy is our Number one Export

The United States produces more democracy than any other country in the world. In fact, we produce more democracy than we need, and we have a surplus. By increasing democracy at home, we create more democracy in the world. That is how democracy became our number one export. There is an increasing need for democracy in the world, so we are constantly exporting it.

We like to promote democracy and that we care about its tenets such as free expression of discontent, civilian government control, voting, rights, and so on. We need to ensure we are democratic by having compliant governments overseas that do what we want. As long as governments act in the interests of the United States, they have free reign over their hen house. That explains our support of the Shah of Iran and Ferdinand Marcos. It also explains our involvement in the assassination of democratically elected Jacobo Arbenz in Guatemala in 1954 and ouster of President elect Jean-Bertrand Aristide from Haiti in September 1994. We do it to protect democracy.

Democracy is like economic growth. You need economic growth just like you need democracy. If you have too much economic growth, it leads to bad things like inflation and wage increases. In the same way, too much democracy leads to bad times on the farm. That's also why we have to export it. Democracy sometimes rises up to the point where people feel that they can protest. People misuse their free speech because they think it might change things. Some of the consequences of too much democracy include the populist movement in the early 1900s that almost destroyed our country and the hippie uprising in the sixties.

People in a democracy vote and have rights. That's why we've created voting machines and the Patriot Act. These are just two of the tools of democracy that we use along with the military, the FBI, CIA, NSA, the World Bank and International Monetary Fund (IMF) and other national and international institutions that promote our style of democracy around the world. Democracy is also improved in this country by donating to political campaigns and gerrymandering districts. We are so democratic that we have even given corporations rights.

The chants of "we're number one" can be heard from Fort Benning, Georgia (School of the Americas) to Guantanamo Prison, to El Salvador and Cambodia, and rightfully so. All over the world people know we have the best democracy and we are the model, much like the Romans and the British before us. I salute our number one export, for without the United States leading the charge, democracy would be dead in the world. We have exported more democracy than anyone, ever.

Using carrot and stick diplomacy, we have enticed countries to follow our lead, or else we have gently beaten them into submission if they didn't act as we told them and become democratic. Obviously, no one else cares as much about the democracy budget as we do. We spread our democracy by intervening in countries that got elections wrong, countries that are hurting their people in ways we don't approve, and countries that don't really know how to be good little trading partners for every God fearing American. From Albania to Zimbabwe, we comb the world looking for opportunities to spread democracy.

Our democracy goes from sea to shining sea. With Manifest Destiny, our God given right to own the land from the Atlantic to the Pacific, we made sure that democracy would spread across our great continent. With the Monroe Doctrine, we have protected democracy for our neighbors in the Western Hemisphere.

We love to spread democracy in the Americas. President James Monroe addresses Congress with his *Monroe Doctrine* in 1823. It was a warning to Europe to stay out of the affairs of the Americas. We even intervened when things went wrong in this hemisphere to help with the democratic processes in countries like Haiti, Nicaragua, Bolivia and many more. That is how much we love to spread democracy around.

We monopolize the media to support democracy. We help reporters defend democracy by only inviting them to "essential events" and giving them content if they want to write about a government event or war. We'll even review the writing for reporters, thus eliminating the need for editors. By controlling the media message, we can ensure the press remains democratic.

Support the Supporter in Chief

We conservatives support our troops. Just look at the millions of U.S. flags wedged in car windows, yellow magnetic ribbons on tailgates, and decals and stickers on car bumpers all over the country. I'll tell you now: we conservatives support our troops. All that paraphernalia proves how much troop supporting there is in this great nation. In 2003, troop supporter in Chief, President Bush, along with his Republican Congress, tried to support our troops in many ways.

First, the Bush administration tried to cut seventy-five dollars a month from the imminent danger pay for soldiers fighting in Iraq. As we know, there is no danger in Iraq now that our mission is accomplished. The 2003 White House budget had tried to cuts three billion dollars from Veteran's because the Executive Branch supports our troops. Bush is fiscally conservative and didn't want to run up the debt buying unnecessary equipment like Kevlar body armor for the soldiers in Iraq, so he didn't.

However, the Democrats and some liberal Republicans in the House of Representatives voted against these cuts 2004 budget. But that didn't stop Bush. Bush knows that troops are in such good health that they don't need health care. Just look at Walter Reed Hospital, for it's the best hospital our troops need. Why spend a lot on health care for healthy people.

God wants us to win this crusade in the Middle East, whatever the cost. Therefore, we will do what it takes to support our troops. We understand that our companies need to make huge profits from the war. We are for the families of the troops in Iraq, so we do what we can to keep the troops in harms way. That's because we want the killing to happen over there, not over here.

The Beginning of Democratic Expansion

Since the Constitution was ratified, the United States has been exporting democracy. The first to take our idea of democracy was the French. They didn't go for it right away, but France finally became democratic in between 1789 and 1799 during the French Revolution. France became even more democratic when Napoleon Bonaparte came to power.

Napoleon took his army to invade and help expand democracy in foreign lands using the military as we do today. In 1802, he became Consul for Life in France. Then on May 18, 1804 Napoleon Bonaparte was proclaimed the French Emperor. From his truly democratic post, he democrified Belgium, Holland, Spain, Italy, and parts of Russia. Unfortunately, the Russian royal family of Czars, with the help of the English, fought back and he could not democrify them. Even though Napoleon failed to democrify all of Europe, his military-democratic expansion has been a model for the United States ever since.

Industry and Democracy

During the Industrial Revolution, democracy started to expand. Briefly stated, the Industrial Revolution started in England around 1790 and spread to Germany, France, and the U.S. around 1840. Industrialization involved an increase in the use of machinery for production of goods and a mass exodus from the farms to the cities.

The hallmarks of a strong democracy are industrialization, free trade and trade agreements, and corporate personhood. We convinced the public and the media that industrialization leads to, and is the same as, democracy. By linking democracy to industry, we can get people to agree to helping out corporations in America because it's democratic.

Social movements by workers, immigrants, progressives, socialists, women, and others had nothing to do with the increase in voting and other democratic rights. People don't make democracy work, corporations and some governments do. *Never* read Howard Zinn's <u>A People's History of the United States</u> because he is against freedom loving industrialists that brought democracy to America. Zinn mistakenly thinks people have something to do with democracy. Only the Industrial Revolution worked to spread democracy.

The steam engine was developed in England and in 1802 was used to pump water out of mineshafts and increase mine productivity. It didn't matter that the miners in England didn't have the right to vote until 1867. The miners couldn't vote, but they were safer from drowning in the mines. We know that with fewer miners dying in the mines, there was more pressure for them to get the vote.

The Cotton Gin was invented in 1793 so those poor slaves didn't have to pick the seeds out of the cotton anymore. This increased the productivity and eventually, seventy-two years later, meant freedom for the slaves and the right to vote. Since women weren't a big part of the work force until WWI, they didn't get the right to vote until after the Great War. Therefore, war and destruction lead to democracy, just like industrialization leads to democracy. Don't let feminazis convince you that the suffragette movement had anything to do with women getting the right to vote. They are wrong. Case closed!

Textile factories were created in England, and they were the first major industry. Having lots of inexpensive clothing allowed democracy to flourish. Who can vote while you're naked? Granted, the children and women who worked in the textile factories didn't have voting rights at the time and lived in horrible conditions while the factory owners were rich, but that is the price of democracy. If they wanted to get rich, why didn't these women and children open their own factories?

In the 1840s, the railroad became a force in England, and later in America. The railroad allowed more people to travel back and forth and allowed us to

Democracy's Our Number One Export

sell more cows. In the United States, the railroad was particularly important for sending troops out West to democrify the Indians. By bringing in all the Chinese and Irish to build the transcontinental railroad, we were able to tie these workers to company stores and the labor market of the United States. This, of course, leads to democracy.

Companies were so helpful to the workers that they built stores in isolated railroad and mining camps to provide supplies and tools to the workers. The workers sometimes worked for free because they couldn't manage their money properly and ended up owing the company store more than they earned.

Never mind that there was discrimination against the workers, especially the Chinese. This discrimination was only meant to force the Chinese and Irish to act more like us, thus they became more democratic. The important thing is that goods could travel back and forth and more white folks could go out West to civilize the land. It also helped us democrify Mexico by taking land from them in 1848 and helped us gain California with its gold and Texas with its oil. The war against Mexico, like all wars, made us more democratic.

A great day in our history occurred in 1859 when oil was found in Pennsylvania by Edwin Drake. Mr. Drake was looking for a way to help democracy with his discovery; that meant making a lot of money. He soon discovered that you could put the oil in a steam engine as a fuel. So he made sure that engines were created or converted to use this seemingly unending supply of fuel, petroleum. As we have discovered, petroleum has helped us bring democracy to Texas, Mexico, Russia, and especially the Middle East. Only the heathen Venezuelans have yet to be democrified by oil, but we are trying.

As we see in Iraq and Iran, democracy is on the move. The Saudi royal family in Saudi Arabia is very democratic, for a monarchy. Oil, one of the main fuels of the Industrial Revolution, has brought democracy to many parts of the world.

Electricity and the light bulb increased democracy for everyone. It allowed workers to increase their hours of labor beyond daylight to a freedom supporting twelve to sixteen hours a day. They could now work at night and use electronic sewing machines.

Electricity also allowed us to have movies and television, the media of freedom. Just watch John Wayne movies or *Fox News* if you don't believe me. Democracy is soon going to be put into electronic voting machines everywhere, thus increasing our control over democracy. As you know, it's not how technology is used for democracy; it's that technology is used.

A Patriot's Guide to Right-Wing Thinking

The increase in industrial activity allowed England, then the United States, to become the largest democrifying powers in the world. By having such a good industrial base, the United States was able to create weapons to democrify Cuba away from the Spanish and install the democratic Batista into power there (more about him later). A great industrial base also allowed us to democrify Nicaragua and put the democratic Somoza into power. We went about democrifying whole regions because we had better weapon-making machines and wanted to use them for the good of everyone in the Americas.

Definitions of Democracy

In the days after WWII, democracy meant anything that was anti-communist. Since the demise of the Soviet Union, at the hands of Reagan, democracy means anti-terrorism. After WWII, the United States supported dictatorships politically, economically, and militarily. As long as they were or could become anti-Soviet, we would give them weapons. Therefore, when we say we support democracy around the globe, we mean we support anybody who would kill communist, or suspected communists, for us.

Democracy also means that commerce is free and unimpeded by governments and the people's right to food and shelter should be secondary or tertiary. Democracy is a buzzword we can use to mean what we want in order to democrify countries we don't like. As far as we are concerned, the ends always justify the means. We support democracy whatever the cost.

Dictators We've Known and Loved

The Shah of Iran

The Shah of Iran was one of the first post WWII dictators we loved. Shah means "king" in the Iranese that they speak in Iran. After we got rid of King George, and Britain and France stripped their kings and queens of most of their power, we went ahead and installed a king to rule Iran in 1953. The reason is that the Shah was weak and needed our help to stay in power. This helped us make sure we could control their democracy.

In 1953, Iran had a prime minister who wouldn't let the British take what was rightfully theirs: the British oil sitting under the Iranian soil. Therefore, when Mohammed Mosadegh was elected in 1951 to be Prime Minister, we had to get rid of him. You see, he had the best interests of Iranians in mind by trying to nationalize the oil and take it all for the Iranians. That wasn't very democratic of him, was it? What did his selfish attitude get him? It got him exiled! The United States got rid of the Prime Minister and put in a man of real integrity that was willing to do whatever it took to get his people comply with democracy, the Shah.

Torture and killing under the Shah was an attempt to democrify the heathen Iranians. It didn't work. For all the love the Shah showed his people, they exiled him in 1979, and the Ayatollah Khomeini took control (Zepezauer: 2003). We tried to create democracy in Iran, but the people weren't ready.

Saddam Hussein

Saddam Hussein of Iraq was a friend of ours in the 1980s before he went bad in 1990. Hussein was a minor military figure in Iraq until the CIA decided we could use him to get a United States friendly government in Iraq. After having his political opposition assassinated, he became supreme leader of Iraq in 1979 (ibid). What a happy coincidence that he came into power the same year as the Ayatollah in Iran. That meant we could use Saddam Hussein of Iraq as a check against the undemocratic Ayatollah who hated our freedoms and was undemocratic unlike the Shah he replaced.

Saddam Hussein only killed the opposition, and later the Kurds, to help democracy. As part of Saddam's democratic plan, Iraq invaded Iran in 1980 using weapons sold to him by the United States. Later, in 1986, when Iran agreed to support a democratic Nicaraguan movement of Contras by giving money to support death squads there, we sold Iran weapons as well.

We helped Saddam out of the desire to create a democratic Middle East. How could our WMDs, invading Iran, mass killings of Kurds and the opposition in Iraq NOT lead to democracy? We've tried exporting and exporting democracy to Iraq, but yet again, the heathens weren't ready for it. We're in a new round of democracy exports to Iraq since 2003, and it looks like democracy's taking hold.

Ferdinand Marcos

Ferdinand Marcos was our friend in the Philippines, and then he betrayed us. At twenty-one, Ferdinand Marcos was convicted of killing Julio Nalundasan, the man who beat his father in Philippine's first national election. Marcos had to kill his father's opponent to ensure future elections were democratic.

Jimmy Carter, Mr. Habitat for Humanity and Nobel Peace Prize himself, got Marcos an $88 million World Bank loan and helped the democratic leader increase his United States aid by 300%. Then a 1976 Amnesty International report identified eighty-eight government torturers in the Philippines and wrote about how alleged subversives were beaten and tortured by the Marcos government. Even Vice President George Herbert Walker Bush praised Marcos's "adherence to democratic principals and to the democratic processes" (Bernstein, et al).

Anastasio Somoza

Nicaragua, led by the Somoza family, was one our great neighbors until the commies took over. There was this revolutionary, Augusto Sandino, in Nicaragua that somehow thought it a good idea to help defend miners and farmers of Nicaragua against United States exploitation. Anyone who helps workers is obviously a communist. Therefore, the United States Marines invaded in 1912 and put the democratic Somoza into power.

Two generations of Somozas made the country democratic for forty years by torturing and murdering those who disagreed with the way people were being tortured and murdered. The Somozas were so democratic that they all became millionaires. As we have learned, the richer you are the more democratic you are. They were so entrepreneurial that the Junior Somoza was able to sell Nicaraguan blood on the blood market and make $12 million dollars a year (Zepezauer: 2003, pg 220). It takes sweat and blood to create a democracy, so the young Somoza knew what he was doing.

In 1972, an earthquake killed about 20,000 people and left 200,000 homeless in Nicaragua. The Somoza family did their best to seize the disaster aid, sell it, and reinvest it to help the nation. They only took a few million dollars in handling fees. In fact, George W. Bush learned a lot about how to help his people after Katrina by the way the Somoza family dealt with the 1972 earthquake (Zepezauer: 2003).

The sad end to this tale of democracy is that the Sandinista Communist Army for the Hatred of God and all that is Good and Sacred (FSLN) took over the country and started to educate the people and provide health care. This damaged democracy because it interfered with free markets.

Fulgencio Batista

Fulgencio Batista was a great leader in Cuba. He became President of Cuba when the former Army Sergeant took power in a 1932 coup. A coup is when the military decides on the best person is to run things democratically. Then he was President, and that proves he was democratic. Roosevelt (the New Deal commie Roosevelt) thought this dictatorial president was the best person to counteract leftists who wanted Cuban people to run their own country. Batista ruled for a while then left in order to return to overthrow another elected Cuban leader, Carlos Prio Socorras in 1952.

Under Batista, U.S. companies did well and there were no questions about democracy. Batista was so democratic that he let the drug mafia use Cuba for drug dealing and money laundering. Cuba became a popular (and democratic) hot spot for wealthy businessmen and politicians from the United States in the 50s.

Most of the people in Cuba were dirt poor under Batista's rule. However, they lived in a democracy, so everything was okay. Despite Batista's manly firmness, and the backing of the United States, Batista was finally overthrown by our bitter enemy Fidel Castro in 1959.

Now we get to live with the United State's government and Miami's Cuban exile community supporting the idea that Castro overthrew a democratic Batista regime and people lived well under Batista rule. We have to tell people that Batista was democratic because we want this kind of democracy to return to Cuba.

Augusto Pinochet

Augusto Pinochet in Chile was a good friend. General Augusto Pinochet, military leader of Chile once said, "Democracy is the breeding ground of communism" (Bernstein). What Pinochet did when he got rid of the democratically elected President Salvador Allende in 1973 was to get rid of that excess democracy that leads to hippyism and communism.

After 150 years of democracy in Chile, it was time to cool it off with some cleansing of the population, say thirty thousand, who were tortured, killed, and exiled (Amnesty International 1). The U.S. government continued to support Pinochet with international loans because he was forging democracy, and the United States only supports democracies. Pinochet is finally dead, and now we have to worry about another commie like Allende taking over Chile.

Ngo Dinh Diem

Ngo Dinh Diem in Vietnam was the great democratic president in South Vietnam when the commies started to take over in the North in the 1950s. He was better than a commie, no matter how many people he tortured and killed. He was so misunderstood that even President Eisenhower admitted that "had elections been held, possibly 80% of the population would have voted for Ho Chi Minh, the communist leader" (ibid). Diem was assassinated in 1963, and democracy was gone forever from Vietnam. It led to the communist takeover of this once freedom loving land.

Chiang Kai-Shek

Chiang Kai-Shek in China was a great democrat that we supported. Yes, it's hard to believe, but China once had a democracy. He became the President of Taiwan (an island off the Chinese coast) after the Chinese communists kicked him off the mainland in 1949. The United States supported Chiang, and they supported Japanese troops fighting the communists even before WWII had ended.

Chiang was misunderstood for his wanton cruelty, corruption, and decadence (support for democracy), and he did not enjoy the support of the (antidemocratic) Chinese people. So what if 85% of the Chinese population had no say under his rule. Isn't that what democracy is about? Thankfully, we had the fear of communism that led us to support Chang and Taiwan instead of Mainland China ruled by Mao and the communists.

Summary

We would personally like to thank the Heritage Foundation for support of the idea that the United States supports democracy, "A wave of democratic change is spreading around the world, from Afghanistan to Iraq to Ukraine...The promotion of democracy remains an important goal of U.S. foreign policy" (Cohen). Thanks to all the storytellers, and the naïve Americas that have been looking for something to believe in since they learned Santa Claus wasn't real. The United States gets to support democratic dictators that do what we want around the world.

The Reagan Rollback

The Reagan rollback plan was an expansion and redefinition of the Truman doctrine of communist containment. The idea was for the United States to rollback governments that disagreed with us. Using low intensity conflict to avoid the "Vietnam Syndrome", nuclear war, or direct conflict with the Soviets, we could coerce governments into our camp to oppose the Soviets.

Low intensity conflict tactics include counter-insurgency and counter-terrorism. Counter-insurgency was used in Guatemala and contra operations against a standing government as we used in Nicaragua and Afghanistan under the Soviets. Counter-terrorism tactics are used against civilians in the Israel-Palestine conflict, against the drug armies in Colombia and against the Libyan terrorist state. Other tactics include sending in peacekeeping forces and strategic bombing. If the United States can get proxy armies to do their work, all the better.

As we saw in Vietnam and now see in Iraq, it is problematic to use our own soldiers to promote democracy. In Central America we learned that we could promote democracy by using contras or anti-insurgency death squads. We must let the local people promote democracy. All we have to do is train them at the School of the Americas and give them the weapons and logistics to get the job done. I will tell you more about the School of the Americas later in this chapter.

Tools of Democracy

The U.S. has many tools to use to promote and ensure democracy. With these tools and techniques, we have remained a great leader in the promotion of freedom and capitalism around the world.

Patriot Act

The USA PATRIOT Act (Uniting and Strengthening America by Providing Appropriate Tools Required to Intercept and Obstruct Terrorism) was passed in 2001. It allows the democratic forces of the Justice Department to look into your video rentals, library records, what you buy, where you go on the internet, what you say on your phone, and spy on you in all sorts of ways without a warrant. What could be more democratic?

By keeping the courts out of the decision making process of granting warrants for searches and seizures, the Patriot Act allows the police, CIA, FBI, and other police agencies to spy on you where ever and whenever they want. As we know, most judges don't know a thing about laws and the Constitution, so why should they be the people we go to for a warrant.

Limiting freedom at home supports freedom and democracy exports abroad. The more you restrict rights, the more democracy you have. What good would it be if we had to go to the courts every time we disliked what someone did or said? Warrants are an intrusion on our democracy.

Putting Money into Politics

When there is more money in politics, there is more democracy. That is why were against campaign finance reform. As I have proven several times already and as is demonstrated on television and in movies every day, the more money you have, the better you are. Shouldn't the best members of society be able to use their financial advantage to get people elected? Billionaires are the best qualified to rule.

The Bipartisan Campaign Reform Act passed in 2003 was a way to control campaign finance without changing the actual donation system. We really don't need to keep big money out of politics; liberals just keep complaining and we had to shut them up. Money greases the shafts and pistons of government, and these pistons move the valves of industry. What we did was pass a law that addressed the concerns of Americans. That doesn't change the way things are done.

This "Campaign Reform Act" banned soft money or money not used directly in a campaign such as money for issue ads that support a candidate's stance. However, groups and individuals can bundle large donations, and overall spending on campaigns is still unlimited. Elections should cost millions of dollars, and they do. Let's not look at alternatives to the incredible campaign costs and tip the democratic cash cow over.

George W. Bush spent $262,000,000.00 to be elected, and John Kerry spent $248,000,000.00 to lose in 2004. I contend that the more money that is spent on elections, the more democratic they are. That is because the more money in a campaign, the more people hear about the candidates and can chose wisely. More money means more advertising, and this advertising gives us a truthful picture of candidates.

The table below features the national dollar amounts spent by both parties in the 2006 elections according to the Center for Responsive Politics (2006). It shows that Republicans are more democratic because they spend more money on campaigns. It also shows that they are more popular because they received more money in donations.

All National Elections	
2005 - 2006	Total Receipts
Democratic Party	$493,311,599
Republican Party	$598,127,532

Political campaigns are a good way to spend money. Members of the House of Representatives have to start fund raising for their next election as soon as they get into office because they are elected every two years. That means democracy is constantly on the march in America. With no hard money limits, money used directly by a campaign, all it takes is some good bundling to raise millions. It's not like we have sick or unemployed people in America, Katrina to clean up, or wars to pay for.

There really aren't any other options to these outrageous campaigns. It's not like we can use the "public airwaves" to give time to the candidates or force politicians to actually travel and talk to people to get the message across or get candidates to go door to door. No, expensive television and mail campaigns are the ONLY way to run elections.

Drug Wars

One of the greatest tools of democracy is the drug war. By becoming involved in drug operations in third world countries, we can insure they remain or become democratic. We have helped with this noble cause through the drug wars in Afghanistan, Colombia, Bolivia, Cambodia, Nicaragua, Honduras, Mexico, Panama, and here in the United States. It seems like nearly all of Central and South America, as well as Asia, have been helped by the drug wars.

The Opium war in China was a great model for us when it comes to the use of drugs and creating a stable government. The war was started when the Chinese refused to let the British control drugs inside of Chinese territory. The British decided to teach the Chinese a lesson and burned down the summer palaces in Beijing (1860). If only the Chinese had allowed lawful and free trade with the British opium merchants, there wouldn't have been a problem. The same could be said with other nations that have had trouble with drugs; if they only had done what the United States wanted, there wouldn't have been trouble.

The Vietnam War, a great effort in the exportation of democracy that failed because of a cowardly military and traitorous commie loving protesters at home, has been accused of creating drug addicts of our soldiers. Michael Levine tells us in his article, "Mainstream Media: The Drug War's Shills" in the book <u>Abuse Your Illusions</u> that soldiers in Vietnam were taking drugs (Levine 24-38). That's only true if you can trust the word of those thousands of soldiers that came back claiming to be addicted and wanted money from the U.S. for their treatment. The doctors who treated these soldiers also lied to corroborate these stories.

What Levine fails to mention is that soldiers wouldn't have been tempted to do drugs if it weren't for that heathen Vietcong army putting all that stress on the poor undermanned American army. We should sue the Vietnamese commies for creating all these drug addicts. We would, except NO soldiers came back addicted to heroine, so what's the point?

Now you know that the U.S. only wants to help countries on drugs. We do this by giving them tough love by bombing and invading them. Let's look at Bolivia. They had 189 coups before their 1980 drug coup. The drug war allowed the Bolivian president to detain his critics lawfully while at the same time making a few extra dollars for himself as a bonus for being on our side. According to Levine, Bolivian drug production increased dramatically to meet the ever-increasing U.S. demand. So where's the problem? Democracies fight the drug wars with us; democracies are not funded by the drug sales.

The Bolivian government made money off the drug war, but we really don't want to question a Bolivian government that was the most stable in decades by addressing drug sales. What our democratic friends do is up to them.

School of Americas: Exporting Democracy One Student at a Time

The School of Americas (SOA), now called the Western Hemisphere Institute for Security Cooperation or WHISC, started in Panama in 1946. But some commies kicked the school out of there in 1984 under the terms of the Panama Canal Treaty. A few people in Latin America didn't like us either. As SOAWatch online tells us:

> Former Panamanian President, Jorge Illueca, stated that the School of the Americas was the "biggest base for destabilization in Latin America" (SOA online).

However, the Marxist President of Panama didn't like the school because he was undemocratic, envied America, and didn't want us helping his Latin American neighbors. Some liberal peaceniks call the school the "School of Assassins" because they don't see the big picture. Sure, the SOA graduates killed, tortured, maimed, raped, mutilated, disappeared, decapitated, hung, and slaughtered hundreds of thousands of people in Latin America, but that was to defend democracy.

Besides dealing with countries and people who disagree with America, the school teaches techniques that reinforce democratic values. Sniper techniques give average citizens a say in country politics. Psychological warfare techniques, such as water boarding taught at the school, help people in all countries mentally prepare for democracy. Interrogation techniques learned there, such as torture, are part of the due process every American enjoys. Why should we keep these skills from our friends?

Now I have proved that the SOA/WHISC exports democracy. However, there are those that disagree. For example, *School of America's Watch, Human Rights Watch, Amnesty International, United Nations, America's Watch,* and thousands of victims say that SOA/WHISC have caused the deaths of thousands of people. What liberals don't understand is that you have to crack a few eggs if you want to make an omelet, and you have to crack a few heads to make a democracy.

People complain about their techniques, but SOA/WHISC graduates only kill educators, union organizers, religious workers, student leaders, human rights workers, liberal or moderate politicians, and others who work for the rights of the poor. Many patriotic red-blooded Americas would love to do the same here in America. At least we get to pass our desires on to Latin Americans who, by the luck of circumstance, can carry out the type of societal cleansing we all want to do.

Jeanne Kirkpatrick, a true American, commented on the role of war protesters at conservativeforum.org, "The dove of peace has become the ostrich of complacency." That proves that if we get rid of SOA/WHISC, we will all become ostriches under an Islamofacist dictatorship.

Torture, Indefinite Detentions and Rendition: Getting at the Truth

Torture is another tool we use to spread democracy. When being tortured, most people decide that they love us and can't wait to put in a presidential government that supports the United States. Our allies such as the Shah of Iran, Marcos in the Philippines and Pinochet in Chile, and countless others trained at SOA/WHISC used torture, and we know how democratic they were. We only use good torture, and the Islamofascists and communists use bad torture.

The Guantanamo Detention Center in Cuba is a laboratory of democracy. Interrogators use torture at Guantanamo, and that proves they are a democratic institution. They have also detained citizens and foreigners there without charging them with a crime, without having evidence against them that would hold up in civilian court, and without giving them access to a lawyer. Terrorist suspects are held without the basic rights rapists and serial killers, who have been caught red-handed, get in the United States. That's because rape and killing are not terrorism.

There was once a thing called the Constitution. There was also something called the Sixth Amendment that stated, "The accused shall enjoy the right to a speedy and public trial." However, the President and all his men had a better idea. Although the Sixth Amendment said nothing about there being exceptions in times of war, for national security, or for "enemy combatants", President Bush decided to detain some suspects without setting trial dates. That means there have been no speedy trials for these suspects. We know that freedom isn't free, and that freedom is a zero sum game; for us to be free, we need to take freedoms away from others.

The Sixth Amendment also says defendants get a lawyer before being interviewed or before they go to trial. Why should terrorism suspects get a lawyer before a trial? A lawyer would train the terrorists how to lie at their trial. We gave these suspects in Guantanamo, Bagram Airbase in Afghanistan, and other places around the world some special treatment. This treatment was given in order to get democracy moving in the war on terrorism.

There was also that Eighth Amendment we had to ignore because it says there shouldn't be cruel and unusual punishments inflicted on the accused. The Constitution states that these rights apply to all people living in the United States, regardless of citizenship status. That didn't matter. Furthermore, we didn't torture people in Guantanamo, no matter what the photos of torture victims and witnesses say. We just gave those suspects a love tap and put them in yoga positions to keep them in shape.

What the government needed after 9/11 was to put forth an impression that progress was being made, so we arrested and detained terrorism suspects. With a few arrests, Bush could say that progress was being made in the war on terror. It didn't matter that no indictments or convictions were being obtained, it just mattered that we were doing something. Congress is supposed to approve any exceptions to the legal rights of detainees, but Congress would have just let the President do what he wanted anyway. So they left it up to the "decider" to decide.

After the 9/11 bombing on America, the Bush Team decided to get rid of judicial influence with regards to criminal prosecutions of terrorists. We scooped up about 660 terrorist suspects without cause, started spying on people's banking, credit card, library, internet, and other records without warrants, and moved on. Warrants would require facts and evidence, something our democracy doesn't know what to do with.

Getting a warrant would take a couple of hours if you actually had evidence, and in those two hours, something might happen. It would take much longer if you didn't have any evidence. Even though the police could act right away if there were an immediate threat, they still would need a warrant just to arrest people if there wasn't an immediate threat (Mayer).

The government also spread democracy by shipping terrorist suspects around the world in an act called "extraordinary rendition". This means that suspected terrorists can be sent to say, Syria, where they will be interrogated by people who know how to use extraordinary means to get information. This is used when the United States can't fully torture a suspect and needs to send him to a country where he can be duly processed (ibid).

Suspects like the four Bosnian terrorist suspects (Page versus Lawyer Committee) who were released in 2002 from prison in Bosnia for lack of evidence were also transferred to Guantanamo. They are under U.S. supervision there but not U.S. court jurisdiction. We don't hear much about them because they're from Bosnia, a country full of Muslims that most Americans can't find on a map. Because they're from Bosnia, we know they're guilty.

There is also the case of Maher Arar, a Canadian citizen, who was caught at JFK Airport on September 26, 2002 as he was switching planes to go to Tunisia. He was on an American watch list. We knew he was guilty because his name was Maher, he was traveling to Tunisia, he was traveling in September (the same month 9/11 happened), and he was switching planes in New York where the terrorist attack occurred on 9/11. We sent him to Syria for some questioning.

A year later he was released from detention because the Canadians said he should be released. He was never connected to actual terror plots, but who knew? We could have just talked to the Canadians about it first, but they would have tried to stop the extradition. Besides, Canadians wouldn't have found out the truth using regular police work like checking phone records, looking into travel to the Middle East, or getting a warrant to tap his phones. No, the only way was to send him to Syria where they would torture him (Mayer). He was beaten, which is true, but we had to make sure we really didn't have any hard evidence on him before we let him go.

Then there was the case of the Egyptian born Australian citizen, Mamdouh Habib. He was caught in Pakistan in October 2001. We knew he was guilty because his name is *Habib*, he was caught in Pakistan, a Muslim county, and he was traveling in October 2001, a month *after* the 9/11 attacks. You see, we can do anything we want after 9/11 because we were hurt. The upshot of the story is that he was sent to Egypt, where they used torture to find out he was innocent (ibid). They let him stay there for three years without charging rent. Torture allows us to find out if people are guilty or not, so it's useful.

I've also seen how torture works really well on television and the movies in getting people to talk, so it must work. Second, we're pissed off and have the right to torture, maim, and kill people unrelated to the terrorist attacks of 9/11 because we're hurting inside and someone has to pay. Kalid Sheikh Mohammed, who really is guilty of planning the 9/11 attacks, couldn't have been caught without torturing thousands of innocents or by using regular police methods.

We justify torture by explaining to people it works. We increase democracy because if someone is rendered to a place where they might be executed, they will disappear and no longer interfere with our government. We know they were all out to get the United States, so that makes them enemy combatants who we can treat how we want.

Even though rendition and torture improve our democracy, there are some so-called experts out there that think torture doesn't lead to confession and are against it.

- Rear Admiral (retired) John Hutson is against torture just because he thinks "'cruel, inhuman or degrading conduct, are not part of our national character'" (Amnesty International 1). What does he know? He was an Admiral. He probably never left his ship to deal with real terrorists!
- Bob Baer, former CIA official, thinks that torture just scares people, but you never get the truth out of the CIA. He thinks the only thing we might get is false confessions. Well Bob, maybe we want to scare them, and then make up our own truth later. Ever thought of that?
- Lawrence Korb, former Naval Intelligence officer and Assistant Secretary of Defense during the Reagan Administration, thinks that if we torture the enemy, they will feel okay torturing us. The man acts as if he has children in the military. Calm down there buckaroo! If you don't have kids in the military, then don't worry about our troops getting tortured. If he thinks our troops can't handle torture better than the towel-heads, then he supports terrorists.
- Michael Scheuer, formerly a senior CIA official in the Counter-Terrorism Center, thinks that by torturing a suspect, he's going to just spill his guts and tell us "'whatever you want to hear.'" Isn't that the point?
- Dan Coleman, retired FBI agent, tells us that by torturing others we might "'lose our souls'" (ibid). Who made him God?

All these so-called experts from military intelligence, the CIA and the FBI don't know anything about terrorism. If they did, they would know that torture helps us feel superior to others. The knowledge that terrorists are being tortured, despite the fact it might not work, keeps up the morale of the soldiers in the field and the folks back home.

Israel: Fighting for Democracy One Bomb at a Time

Anybody who points out any wrong that Israel may have ever committed is fighting against the United States. Israel is the main proponent of our type of democracy in the Middle East. If a country agrees with us, and they use planes to bomb a common foe, they are democratic. If a people or country uses suicide attacks and car bombs on people, like the Palestinians, they are undemocratic.

Israel, much like the United States, believes that democracy has to be earned. Israel exports democracy to Palestine and neighboring countries like we do in Latin America. By putting concerns of security over human rights, Israel can justify democrifying the Palestinians violently and using armed attacks against noncombatants. Through their control of water resources, and their advanced stock of U.S. weaponry, Israel is in the best position to share its democracy with the region.

According to a 2006 Amnesty International report on Palestinian Territories, army roadblocks, walls, checkpoints and other travel restrictions imposed on Palestine by the Israeli army in the Occupied Territories cause up to 50% unemployment. In 2006, Israeli forces killed about 190 Palestinians, including around fifty children. The Israeli military attacked the Palestinian territories, Lebanon, and anybody else they didn't like. It was done to impose some sense of democracy in the region. Israel also violently attacked peace demonstrations to quell the uprising of undemocratic forces (Amnesty International 2).

Israeli settlers frequently attacked Palestinian farmers in 2006, destroying orchards and preventing cultivation of their land. The Israeli Army killed Palestinians with the help of Jewish settlers. At the same time, Israel said they would stop the settlements. Arresting people faster than doctors kill babies in the United States, Israeli officers did their best to make sure no one would be left in the territories to turn the settlers away.

In 2006, democratic forces in Israel didn't take the bait and work for an "Irish Type Peace" that gives some power to the religious minority in the region. My God, can you imagine what an employed Palestinian workforce that has decent lives would do? Israel would have no one to fear and no way to justify the billions of dollars the United States gives Israel each year. The Israeli people might object to killing Palestinians and peace might break out. The religious conservatives run the government in Israel, so peace is not near.

How to Promote Democracy

Democracy is so important, that we must force it down the throats of the world and the American people. Here's how we do it and will continue to do it under President John McCain.

1. POWERFUL AND CONTINUING NATIONALISM –
In order to enforce truly democratic rule in America, we need to make constant use of patriotic mottos, slogans, symbols, songs, and other paraphernalia. Flags are seen everywhere as are flag symbols on clothing and in public displays.

2. REDEFINITION OF HUMAN RIGHTS -
We need to use fear of enemies and the need for security to persuade the people that human rights can be ignored in certain cases because of "need". The people tend to look the other way or even approve of torture, summary execu-

tions, assassinations, long incarcerations of prisoners, if we fear a threat. As I proved in this chapter, all of these techniques promote democracy.

3. IDENTIFICATION OF ENEMIES/SCAPEGOATS AS A UNIFYING CAUSE –

The people are rallied into a unifying patriotic frenzy over the need to eliminate a perceived common threat or foe to democracy such as racial, ethnic or religious minorities, liberals, communists, socialists, and terrorists. Fear makes our democracy possible.

4. SUPREMACY OF THE MILITARY –

Even when there are widespread domestic problems, the military is given a disproportionate amount of government funding, and the domestic agenda is neglected. Soldiers and military service are glamorized in order to protect democracy.

5. RAMPANT SEXISM –

Our democratic government should be exclusively male-dominated. Real democracies recognize that only men truly understand how to run a country. Traditional gender roles are made more rigid. Divorce, abortion, and homosexuality are suppressed, and the state is represented as the ultimate guardian of the family institution.

6. CONTROLLED MASS MEDIA -

Media is a tool of democracy as long as you control it. Therefore, media should be directly an arm of the government, or at least indirectly controlled by government regulation, sympathetic media spokespeople, corporations, and CEOs. Censorship is unnecessary when you own the media.

7. OBSESSION WITH NATIONAL SECURITY -

Fear is used as a democratic motivational tool by the government over the masses.

8. RELIGION AND GOVERNMENT ARE INTERTWINED –

Our democratic government must use the most common religion in the nation as a tool to shape public opinion. Religious rhetoric and terminology is common from government leaders, even when the major tenets of the religion are diametrically opposed to the government's policies or actions. Without religion, people wouldn't have a moral compass, and they might have to think for themselves.

9. CORPORATE POWER IS PROTECTED –

The industrial and business aristocracy of our democratic nation are the ones who put the government leaders into power, creating a mutually beneficial business/government relationship and power elite while keeping the United States vital for all of its citizens.

10. LABOR POWER IS SUPPRESSED –
Because the organizing power of labor is liberal at best and communist at worst, it is the only real threat to our democratic government. Labor unions should be either eliminated or severely suppressed.

11. DISDAIN FOR INTELLECTUALS AND THE ARTS –
Our democratic nation has no need for higher education for a majority of the population. That is why we must keep universities expensive. Most professors and other academics should be censored or even arrested. Free expression in the arts and letters should be openly attacked. We must arrest Bill Moyers.

12. OBSESSION WITH CRIME AND PUNISHMENT –
Our democracy must focus on crime that the common people commit and give the police limitless power to enforce laws. The people will be willing to overlook police abuses and even forego civil liberties in the name of patriotism. Our democracy needs a national police force with virtually unlimited power. Dick Cheney should run this police force with the help of the Gambino family. Mussolini got help from the mafia to run Italy, why shouldn't we?

13. RAMPANT CRONYISM AND CORRUPTION –
Our democracy should be governed by groups of friends and associates who appoint each other to government positions and use governmental power and authority to protect their friends from accountability. Our national resources and treasures should be appropriated and given to government leaders. Corruption will only be used to strengthen our democracy.

14. FRAUDULENT ELECTIONS –
Sometimes elections in our democracy must be manipulated by smear campaigns against, or even assassination of, opposition candidates, use of legislation to control voting numbers or political district boundaries, and manipulation of the media. Faulty voting machines and eliminating minorities from the voting roles will also protect our democracy. We must use our judiciary to manipulate or control elections when democracy is threatened.
By Tex Shelters adapted from Allen L. Roland's *What is Fascism?* at www.allenroland.com.

Conclusion: We're Number One

We promote more democracy than anyone else, and we're the most democratic nation on earth. If you don't believe me, we'll arrest you and torture you until you do. We are only thinking of others when we put dictators into power in the world. It's tough love like that that leads us to be a true democratic state.

There are other democracies in the world, but where would they be without us? England and France both had their bacon saved from the fire by us in World War II. So did the rest of Europe. Let's forget about the times when other countries helped us, like the French helping us defeat the English in the Revolutionary war. That goes against the truth of U.S. self-sufficiency. The greatest country in the world doesn't need to work with the lesser nations. What really makes us unique is that our number one export is not cars, cell phones, clothing, or even weapons. Democracy is our number one export.

Do Not to Get Involved

One reason I wrote this book is my desire to tell you what a dangerous time it is in America. One of the biggest dangers is citizen involvement. If you get involved, you hate America and will be called unpatriotic. Those names hurt and sting. If you don't want our vicious name-calling directed at you by Ann Coulter or myself, just don't get involved. There are a lot of people getting involved, and what does it do for them? Well, let me tell you what registering voters, educating yourself and others, and helping people in need will do for you.

First off, if you help others, you will have a sense of well being. If you feel good about yourself, you spend less, and the economy might collapse. Just don't do it. Remember how the media makes you feel worthless. Now, if you go shopping, you'll feel better and be better.

I also beg you, please, don't help the environment! If you get involved in roadside clean up or planting trees, things will only get worse. People will see clean roads as an invitation to pollute even more. Reagan once said, "Trees cause pollution." You would only hurt the planet by cleaning it and helping it grow.

Don't think about helping people in your town. By helping people you don't know, you might be less afraid of others. I am here to tell you that people will hurt you. If you work with others and cooperate, you only set yourself up for more hurt. The Homeland Security Department was established to enhance the fear people feel. If you don't feel the fear right away, before you even know someone, you will get hurt. Just lock your doors, stay inside, keep away from everyone (including the pizza delivery guy) and everything will be all right. If you insist on ordering takeout, leave your money on the stoop and tell them to leave the pizza and step away from the door with their hands up.

Getting involved is time consuming. There are more important things to do than visiting AIDS patients, taking a fatherless boy out for a day, visiting people in transitional housing or helping people with disabilities. Instead, you could be watching celebrity boxing, drinking alone, eating at Hooters, or participating in any other valuable pastime. The reason we want you to work at least two jobs is that two jobs won't leave you any time to ruin the country by helping out your neighbor.

Finally, getting involved requires hope. Hope is such a hard, tiring thing to have. Helping one person doesn't change the world, so why bother. If you help others, it hurts the power elite and Billionaires. If you care about Enron CEOs, the heads of the Forbes 500, politicians who give the richest 1% millions of dollars in tax cuts, you have to stop helping average citizens right now. Stop before you read this sentence, and get others to stop getting involved. The worst way to show you have hope is by voting, so don't do it.

Fear is good for America

I hope you're now sufficiently afraid of the future, of terrorism, of immigrants, and of others that I don't have to remind you how dangerous it is out there. Now don't pay attention to economic downturns or environmental disasters, because any day now, some group will get you with a dirty bomb, dirty needles, or dirty socks. Now that is what you need to be a fearing. You must be constantly vigilant when it comes to random events that are unlikely to happen to you and that you have no control over.

Remember dear reader, you are responsible for your own list of fears. Don't let the Attorney General catch you without your fear in hand. Perhaps you have your fear in hand as you read this page?

Now that you've read the book, you understand how much liberals hate America and love terrorists. Liberals should be so ashamed after reading this book that they become conservatives. If you're a liberal, convert now. I am waving my autographed copy of the "How to Talk to a Liberal" while looking at Ann Coulter's picture. I write this with one hand and have my fear in the other hand. To convert and renounce all things un-American and liberal, repeat the following oath 40 days and 40 nights as you cry yourself to sleep over the loss of the Clinton Presidency.

United States Corporagovernment Liberal Conversion Loyalty Oath

- I am of sound mind and renounce all liberal leanings.
- I will stop whining at my fate and start scowling at the poor and helpless, even if they include family and friends.
- I will stop thinking about world crises and tragedies and start thinking about world domination.
- I swear to hate non-conservatives and stop listening to other opinions.
- I will put Rush Limbaugh on my radio and rip off the knob.
- Fox News and ESPN Sports will be my only sources of television news.
- I swear to cheer every time a former sports star dies senselessly in Iraq, ala Pat Tillman.
- I swear to trade in my VW Bug, VW Van, or Toyota Prius for an SUV and blame gas prices on tree huggers who don't want us to spoil Alaska with oil drilling.
- I swear to denounce the killing of unborn children while supporting cuts in Kids-Care, AID to Families, Head Start, childcare, and any other programs that waste money helping poor children.
- While defending life, I will support the killing of doctors that give safe abortions to the middle class and poor and I swear to support the rich while they choose to get illegal, expensive, but safe abortions for their families after we repeal Roe versus Wade.
- I swear not to speak unless spoken to and not to vote unless told to vote.
- I understand that it is never the President's fault, nor are conservatives to blame for the failing economy, the war in Iraq, the loss of jobs, nor anything else that goes wrong under their watch. I understand that if I blame them, the Patriot Act might be invoked and I could be severely punished.

Name_____

Signature_____

Copy and mail to Tex Shelters, Care of Baker Street Press Tucson, AZ 85732-3866

Epilogue
How Right-Wing thinking is Right

Government is too big and it's the liberals' fault. As Ann Coulter says, "If Clinton had his way, welfare mothers would be running this country". Well, it's something she might say. Being that Clinton grew up poor in Arkansas to a single hussy, we know that Clinton naturally dislikes the well to do. At the same time, he is a rich elitist liberal. Who else could be so devilishly clever to hate the rich and be rich himself? Clinton was a double threat to us, and thank God that God had the sense to elect Bush to clean up Clinton's mess.

The worst thing Clinton tried to do was fix health care. It's a good thing we got the liberal media to make up some things for us Billionaires before Clinton's health care plan got off the ground. Imagine letting the poor get sick without paying full price. They can get all the meds they need at Wal-Mart. If the poor can't afford getting sick, why do they insist on doing so? Like my Granddad said, "If you can't pay the pig, don't eat the slop."

Through government propaganda and Billionaire support, democracy has oozed like a petroleum spill throughout the Middle East and the world. Sure, some people have gotten hurt in the oily transition to democracy, but that's a small price to pay for an American style democracy. Our democracy is the worst of them all, except for all the others.

We lead the way in rights reductions, official incarcerations, income disparity, and all the hallmarks of a great democracy. Our democracy includes low wages, low literacy rates, union busting, media monopolies, good schools for only good people (the rich!), bad schools for loser families, and so forth. We have shown countries that fear is a great way to rule. Just look at what fear has done for the democracies of Iraq, Panama, Egypt, Israel, Bolivia, Kenya, Panama, Mexico, Colombia, Russia, Paraguay and other great democracies of the world. For more on how these countries are great democracies, go to transperancy.org.

Billionaires and their government minions love to create programs that protect our wealth and cut programs that do not. We are fiscally responsible, and we save money by cutting programs that protect everyone else. We have such clever names for these programs too: "Clear Skies Initiatives", "Healthy Forests", and so on.

We reduced the size of government by reducing individual rights. There are too many rights and we should cut that Bill of Rights down to two Amendments: the Second (guns) and the Tenth Amendments (states rights).

A Patriot's Guide to Right-Wing Thinking

The first thing we have to do is eliminate the free-speech zones. Liberal protestors are herded in areas called free-speech zones, away from the patriotic crowds at Republican conventions and trade meetings, and allowed to speak freely where the press can't hassle them. These zones put so many burdens on the American people by forcing them to think. Let's get rid of free speech in general; why burden the populace with speech they don't know how to use. Cutting out free speech helps us save money on education.

It is also great to see how much time and media attention is given to prayer in school while Congress (Billionaire collection agents) takes money out of the schools and puts it into our no-bid contracts in Iraq. Certainly, fighting to change separation of church and state into the embedded church and state is worth a few dollars. It certainly raises the cackles of those "free speech" nuts that can't stop us from stealing from the till as they scamper to prevent a school takeover by the religious right.

Our own private army of fundamentalists in the schools, in the courts, in Congress, and in the White House guarantees that Billionaires have the smoke screen of Christianity while we steal from the poor and give to ourselves. That is exactly what Christ had in mind when he fed the hungry on the Sabbath. By creating low wage jobs, Billionaires are surely doing the work of Jesus. God allows us to steal from the poor as a way to help them. Here is a story that exemplifies how the rich suffer for the poor from the parable of Lazarus, Luke 16:19-31:

> There was a rich man, who was clothed in purple and fine linen and who feasted sumptuously every day. And at his gate lay a poor man named Lazarus, full of sores, who desired to be fed with what fell from the rich man's table; moreover the dogs came and licked his sores. The poor man died and was carried by the angels to Abraham's bosom. The rich man also died and was buried; and in Hades, being in torment, he lifted up his eyes, and saw Abraham far off and Lazarus in his bosom.

The rich man suffered in luxury, ate until sated, was prevented from hard labor, and was forced to wear fine clothes so Lazarus could get into the Kingdom of Heaven. He also allowed Lazarus to eat scraps from his table without having to work for them. The poor should thank the Billionaires, like the rich man from the parable, for helping make life and the passage to the afterlife, easy and expedient for the poor.

Here on earth, we can get rid of the rights to a fair trial. It's just too expensive to pay lawyers to defend people we all know are guilty. The idea of a speedy trial is also a detriment to real justice. Shouldn't prosecutors have all the time they need to make a case against the accused? Shouldn't the police have sufficient time to fabricate realistic evidence? Wouldn't we all be safer if indefinite detentions were the norm?

While we might allow a few rights to those in the United States that pass loyalty oaths, jealous foreigners should not have any rights at all. They all want to take away my wife, dog, truck and mansion as well as your jobs and rights. They want to take it all from you. You need to understand that foreigners are the reason Americans lose jobs, lose houses, lose spouses, lose pets, and lose baseball games.

Foreigners are all money grubbing invaders who take and take and take. How dare they come over here and work harder than us. They are lazy welfare-cheating foreigners. It's because of those immigrants that we don't get to export all the jobs overseas that we want. Illegal immigrants, by their very presence, force us to give them jobs. They're stealing your stuff. Go and get them ye olde Minutemen. Thanks for not targeting cheap outsourcing by corporations as liberals tell you to do.

All we have to do is make sure our media conglomerates cover this border clash while we write new laws for Congress to send more jobs overseas. You see, it's legal to send jobs overseas; we're only sending jobs overseas to keep from hiring those illegals and breaking the law. It's not our fault if Americans aren't willing to live in squalor to keep their jobs.

While the poor misbehave and remain poor, Billionaires remain models for human behavior and morality. We are so content because we have everything we want. Why don't you go and buy what you really want right now. If you don't have the latest cell phone, a new car, and 500 channels on your HD TV, you better get out there soon. If you didn't *need* more credit cards, new phones or new cable contracts for your home and other services that you never heard of, people wouldn't be calling you to offer them. There are plenty of things that you don't have. Thankfully, there are businesses that are willing to help you fulfill these needs. That is what businesses do; they fulfill needs. Billionaires are just a cog in the great wheel of need fulfillment.

The upshot is you have to have to consume to feel good about yourself. The American economy is based on consumption. Therefore, the more you buy, the more patriotic you are. That's why Christmas, not the Forth of July, is the most patriotic holiday. What really irks me is how wealthy elite Democrats refuse to buy luxury vehicles and SUVs. Why, when they could buy a new vehicle, do they insist on having their old car repaired and serviced? It's selfish.

A Patriot's Guide to Right-Wing Thinking

The reason car manufactures are doing so poorly in America is poor consumerism.

One reason we must insist on making bankruptcy more difficult is that people aren't consuming enough. If they only consumed more, they would have more, and they could get more credit and not worry about that pesky debt. I don't see why people don't realize this. Some of your pockets are tighter than bark on a yew tree.

The government has been living by increasing the debt ceiling every year (except for a couple of those Clinton years), and individuals should take more credit to avoid debt as well. Forget saving. We must increase spending as a way to keep our economy rolling and feel good about ourselves.

America is number one because we know it is true. It is true because we have more toys than anyone else. We have more bombers, stealth and otherwise, more cruise missiles, more attack cruisers on the sea, and more nuclear weapons. This gives us pride. We also eat more fast food, have more X-Boxes, and have the highest per capita number of movie theaters, televisions, game boys, music stores, and other necessities of life.

We're imperfect, but in America, that's no problem. We can buy our way to happiness. You have all sorts of blemishes and faults. That is why we have blemish cream, aging cream, pimple cream, skin cream (face, body, feet, eye, neck, buttocks, bosom, etc), extra firming day cream, extra firming night cream, day/night lifting cream, shaving cream, stress recovery cream, progesterone (hormone) cream, spot cream, tanning cream, burn cream, stretch cream, breast enhancement cream, penis enhancement cream, itch cream, hair cream, cream rinse, hair removal cream, hair restoring cream, varicose vein cream, and for total stress reduction, ice cream. So, whatever the need, there's a cream. Democracy in America is safe as long as you know that whatever problem you have, there's a cream for it.

In order to meet the needs of America, we need to buy, buy, buy. We don't want to limit our consumption to goods in the United States; we need foreign goods, too. The world also needs our goods. Democracy depends on a free exchange of ideas, electronic games, plastic toys, and Hollywood movies. Without free trade, none of this would be possible and democracy would be threatened. The best way to make trade free is by letting the world's leading capitalist nations make up all the rules for the rest of the world. Who better to tell people what to do than the United States with the help of Europe and Japan? The United States has been successfully using up the world's resource for years now, so we should be in charge of setting the rules for selling what is left.

With Billionaires in charge anything is possible. We will continue to keep America great and the envy of the whole world. There is no reason to get involved in anything except consuming. Voting doesn't count, so why do it? Go home, watch television, and let us get on with the job of running things. God bless *our* America.

A Patriot's Guide to Right-Wing Thinking

Bibliography

Aaron, Craig. "The Medicare Drug War: An Army of Nearly 1,000 Lobbyists Pushes a Medicare Law that Puts Drug Company and HMO profits Ahead of Patients and Taxpayers." Public Citizen Congress Watch. 2004. June 30, 2007 <http://www.citizen.org/documents/MedicareDrugWarReportREVISED72104.pdf>.

Alterman, Eric. What Liberal Media? The Truth About Bias and the News. New York: Basic Books, 2003, 2004.

Amnesty International 1. "Military, Intelligence and Law Enforcement Officers Opposing Torture." 2006. March 7, 2007 <http://www.amnestyusa.org/stoptorture/officersquotes.html>.

Amnesty International 2. "Amnesty Report on the Occupied Territories." 2006. November, 8 2006 <http://www.amnestyusa.org/countries/israel_and_occupied_territories/document.do?id=ar&yr=2006>.

Anniston Star, The "Reed spreads loot, not Gospel." June 24, 2006. In our opinion: Editorials. Sept. 1, 2006 <http://www.politicalparlor.net/wp/2006/06/page/2/>.

Arm Chair Subversive. "Republican Hypocrisy Revealed: Stop Republican Peophelia." 2006. October 2006 <http://www.armchairsubversive.com/>.

Associate Press. "Partial birth abortion' ban struck down: Third ruling against law sets stage for Supreme Court showdown." 2004. MSNBC Nov. 13, 2006 <http://www.msnbc.msn.com/id/5941648/>.

Barkin, Joel. The Corporation: The Pathological Pursuit of Profit and Power. New York, New York: Free Press, 2004.

Beach, William W. 1. "Time to Eliminate the Costly Death Tax." Heritage Foundation. Dec 2006 <http://www.heritage.org/Research/Taxes/EM679.cfm>.

Beach, William W. 2. "The 2005 Index of Dependency." 2005. The Heritage Foundation. Dec 7, 2006 <http://www.heritage.org/Research/Budget/cda05-05.cfm>.

Berkowitz, Bill. "War on Christians?" March 22, 2006. December 19, 2006 <http://www.mediatransparency.org/pdastory.php?storyID=117>.

Bernstein, Dennis and Sydel, Laura. "Dictators Supported by the U.S. Government." Friendly Dictators. 1995. Janyuary 5, 2007 <http://www.omnicenter.org/warpeacecollection/dictators.htm>.

Billington, Alex. "Post-Oscar: Forest Whitaker's Brilliant Acceptance Speech." February 26, 2007. March 2007 <http://www.firstshowing.net/2007/02/26/forest-whitakers-acceptance-speech/>

Bloom, Allen. The Closing of the American Mind. New York, New York: First Touchtone Press, 1987.

Brush, Michael "Insiders' sweet stock deals under fire." June 1, 2006. MSN Money online. April 3, 2007 <http://articles.moneycentral.msn.com/Investing/CompanyFocus/InsiderDeals UnderFire.aspx>.

Boehlert, Eric "Fake news, fake reporter." salon.com. April, 24 2007 <http://dir.salon.com/story/news/feature/2005/02/10/gannon_affair/index.html>.

Boese, Wade. "Global Arms Exports Climbed in 2004." Arms Control Today. November 2005 October, 2006 <http://www.armscontrol.org/act/2005_11/NOV-GlobalArms.asp?print>.

Bracey, Gerald W. "No Child Left Behind: Where Does the Money Go?" June 2005 May, 14 2007 <http://epsl.asu.edu/epru/documents/EPSL-0506-114-EPRU.pdf>.

Buchanan, John and Michael, Stacey "Bush Family - Nazi Dealings - WWII to 1951." November 7, 2003. The New Hampshire Gazette Vol. 248, No. 3, November 7, 2003. Third World Traveler. January5,2007 <http://www.thirdworldtraveler.com/Politicians/Bush_Nazi_Dealings.html>.

CBS Moneyline: 2006 March, 3 2007 <http://money.cnn.com/magazines/fortune/fortune500/industries/Pharmaceuticals/1.html>.

Center for Responsive Politics. OpenSecrets.org. 2006. October 12, 2007 <http://www.opensecrets.org/parties/index.asp>.

Central Pacific Railroad Photographic History Museum online "Chinese-American Contribution to the Transcontinental Railroad." May 29, 2007. <http://cprr.org/Museum/Chinese.html>.

CNN.com "Department of Education to tighten Pell Grant eligibility." December 23, 2004. CNN. December 23, 2004 <http://www.cnn.com/2004/EDUCATION/12/23/pell.grants/>.

Cockcroft, James D. Latin America: History, Politics, and U.S. Policy/Second Edition Chicago: Nelson-Hall Publishers, 1996.

Cohen, Ariel Ph.D., and Dale, Helle C. "The ADVANCE Democracy Act: A Dose of Realism Needed." Executive Memorandum #968. Heritage.org. January 2nd, 2007 <http://www.heritage.org/Research/NationalSecurity/em968.cfm >.

Connolly, Ceci and Mike Allen. "Medicare Drug Benefit May Cost $1.2 Trillion Estimate Dwarfs Bush's Original Price Tag." Washington Post. February 9, 2005; Page A01. June 5, 2007 <http://www.washingtonpost.com/wp-dyn/articles/A9328-2005Feb8.html>.

ConservativeForum.org. "Selections from Jean Kirkpatrick." 2006. February 12, 2007. <http://www.conservativeforum.org/authquot.asp?ID=704>.

Cray, Charlie. "No Bid And No Problem." TomPaine.common sense. July 7, 2004. March 10, 2007 <http://www.tompaine.com/articles/no_bid_and_no_problem.php>.

Crichton, Michael "Aliens Cause Global Warming." michaelcrichton.com. January 17, 2003. February 14, 2007. <http://www.crichton-official.com/speeches/speeches_quote04.html>.

De Tocqueville, Alex. Democracy in America. March, 3 2006 <http://xroads.virginia.edu/~HYPER/DETOC/toc_indx.html>.

Dobbs, Michael. "Halliburton's Deals Greater Than Thought." August 28, 2003. Washington Post. June 12, 2007 <http://www.washingtonpost.com/ac2/wp-dyn/A56429-2003Aug27?language=printer>.

Donaldson-Evans, Catherine. "Would-Be Priests Choose 'God or the Girl' on TV, Sort Of." March 30, 2006. Fox News. June 20, 2007 <http://www.foxnews.com/story/0,2933,189741,00.html>.

Eckstein, Ron "Children's Defense Fund Urges Federal Medicaid Officials To Reject Changes to TennCare Program That Will Harm Children." Children's Defense Fund. May 10, 2007 <http://campaign.childrensdefense.org/pressreleases/050401.aspx>.

Ehrenreich, Barbara. Nickeled and Dimed: On (Not) Getting By in America. New York, New York: Henry Holt and Company, 2001.

Epstein, Edward. "Troops in Danger Zones No Longer Face Pay Cut: Pentagon drops plans for scheduled rollback." August 15, 2003. San Francisco Chronicle. July 11, 2007 <http://www.commondreams.org/headlines03/0815-09.htm>.

Farsetta, Diane and Price, Daniel. "Fake TV News: Widespread and Undisclosed: A multimedia report on television newsrooms' use of material provided by PR firms on behalf of paying clients." April 6, 2006. Center for Media and Democracy. Oct. 3, 2006 <http://www.prwatch.org/fakenews/execsummary>.

Federal Reserve Bank. "Federal Reserve Statistical Release: Consumer Credit." 2006. March 10, 2007 <http://www.federalreserve.gov/releases/g19/Current/>.

Finer, Lawrence B., Lori F., Frohwirth, Lindsay, A. Dauphinee, Susheela Singh and Ann M. Moore. "Reasons U.S. Women Have Abortions: Quantitative and Qualitative Perspectives." Perspectives on Sexual and Reproductive Health. 2005. August, 3 2006 <http://www.guttmacher.org/pubs/psrh/full/3711005.pdf>.

Francis, Robert. "Two Kinds of Beings: The Doctrine of Discovery And Its Implications for Yesterday and Today." Manataka American Indian Council. July 2006. <http://www.manataka.org/~manataka/page94.html>.

Friedman, Thomas. The World is Flat: A Brief History of the Twenty-First Century. New York, New York: Farrar, Straus and Giroux, 2005

A Patriot's Guide to Right-Wing Thinking

Fair Action Alert. "A New Blacklist for Excuse Makers: Those who think Iraq War sparks terror are "despicable," says Friedman." Fair Online. July 27, 2005. December, 9 2006 <http://www.fair.org/index.php?page=2598>.

Gerencher, Kristen. "EARNINGS WATCH: Updates, advisories and surprises." 2004. CBS MarketWatch. September, 10 2006 <http://www.marketwatch.com/News/Story/Story.aspx?guid={04A2FC4E-12BE-4E77-B497-72D80479CDB8}&dist=ArchiveSplash&param=archive&siteid=mktw&garden=&minisite=>.

GLAAD. "Monitor and Mobilize." June 9, 1999. GLAAD. February, 9 2007 <http://www.glaad.org/programs/monitor/monitoring.php>.

Glassman, James K. "Certainty of Catastrophic Global Warming is a Hoax." Capitalist Magazine. Dec. 15, 2003. Novermber 5, 2006 <http://capmag.com/article.asp?ID=3400>.

Guthrie, Arlo "Alice's Restaurant Massacree." Alice's Restaurant Warner Reprise Records, 1965.

Habitat for Humanity Fact Sheet Habitat for Humanity Online. 2006. August, 15 2006 <http://www.habitat.org/how/factsheet.aspx>.

Harris, David. "An American Civil Liberties Union Special Report." June 1999. ACLU. May, 3 2007 <http://www.aclu.org/racialjustice/racialprofiling/15912pub19990607.html>.

Hartung, William D. and Donnelley, Ceara. "New Numbers: The Price of Freedom in Iraq and Power in Washington." August 2003. Arms Trade Resource Center. March 13, 2007 <http://www.worldpolicy.org/projects/arms/updates/081203.html>.

Hatecrime.org 2006. August, 5 2006 <http://www.hatecrime.org/subpages/hatespeech/hate.html>.

Herbert, Bob. "Curing Health Costs: Let the Sick Suffer." Commondreams.org. 2005. New York Times. September, 5 2006 <http://www.commondreams.org/views05/0901-22.htm>.

Hinks, Dennis. "God and Creation: Creation & Environment." My Journal. 2006. June 5, 2007. <http://www.journal33.org/godworld/creation.htm>.

Homeland Security. 2006. Usgov. December, 9 2006. <http://www.dhs.gov/dhspublic/display?theme=36>.

Institute for Policy Studies. "New CEO/Worker Pay Gap Study: Labor Day Report Reveals Layoff Leaders Cushioned from Downturn." 2001. The Progress Report. March 23, 2007 <http://www.progress.org/gap01.htm>.

Jehl, Douglas. "Washington Insiders' New Firm Consults on Contracts in Iraq." September 30, 2003. New York Times. February 19, 2007 <http://www.nytimes.com/2003/09/30/politics/30LOBB.html?ex=1175572800&en=100867d67c0d7087&ei=5070>.

Kingston, Jack and Walter Jones. "The Academic Bill of Rights Goes to Washington." Wednesday, October 22, 2003. FrontPageMagazine.com. March

14, 2007
<http://www.frontpagemag.com/Articles/ReadArticle.asp?ID=10444>.

Kirkpatrick, David. "Conservatives Pick Soft Target: A Cartoon Sponge." January 20, 2005. New York Times. January 5, 2007 <http://www.nytimes.com/2005/01/20/politics/20sponge.html>.

Kozol, Jonathan. Savage Inequalities: Children in America's Schools. New York, New York: Harper Perennial, 1991.

Levine, Michael. "Mainstream Media: The Drug War's Shills." Abuse Your Illusions: The Disinformation Guide to Media Mirages and Establishment Lies. 2003. Edited by Kick, Richard. The Disinfomation Company: New York, New York, 2003. 24-38.

Loconte, Joseph. "Why Religious Values Support American Values." September, 26 2005. Heritage Foundation. September 2006 <http://www.heritage.org/Research/Religion/hl899.cfm>.

Mayer, Jane. "Annals of Justice: Outsourcing Justice." 2005. The NewYorker. January 2007. <http://www.newyorker.com/printables/fact/050214fa_fact6>.

Media Matters 1. "The 'Truth' according to Limbaugh: Feminism established 'to allow unattractive women easier access to the mainstream of society'." August 16, 2006. Media Matters. Dec 1, 2007 <http://mediamatters.org/items/200508160001>.

Media Matters 2. "Savage Nation: It's not just Rush; Talk radio host Michael Savage: 'I commend' prisoner abuse; 'we need more'." May 13, 2004. Media Matters. Dec. 1, 2007. <http://mediamatters.org/items/200405130004>.

Media Matters 3. "James Dobson compared Supreme Court justices to the KKK." April 11, 2005. Media Matters. November, 29 2007 <http://mediamatters.org/items/200504110005>.

Metcalf, Stephen. "Reading Between the Lines." 2002. The Nation. October 2006.
<http://www.fairtest.org/nattest/Nation%20piece%20bush%20links.html>.

Microsoft, Encarta Online Encyclopedia. "British Empire." 1997. MSN. September 19, 2007
<http://uk.encarta.msn.com/encyclopedia_761566125/british_empire.html>.

Morgan, Robin. "Fighting Words for a Secular America: Ashcroft & Friends vs. George Washington & The Framers." 2004. Ms. Magazine November 2006. <http://www.msmagazine.com/fall2004/fightingwords.asp>.

Murray, Charles. Losing Ground: American Social Policy, 1950-1980. New York, New York: Basic Books, 1984.

Nader, Ralph. "If Sam's Club Can Negotiate for Lower Pharmaceutical Prices, Why Can't Uncle Sam?." November 28, 2003. CommonDreams.org. June 19, 2007 <http://www.commondreams.org/scriptfiles/views03/1128-07.htm>.

O'Neil, Patrick, Karl Fields, and Don Share. "Political Economy: Mexico." Cases for Comparative Economics. Novemebr, 2006

<http://www.wwnorton.com/college/polisci/compol/demo/economy_mexico.htm>.

Oregon.gov "FAQs about the Death With Dignity Act." Dignity with Death Act. Novemeber, 10 2007. <http://egov.oregon.gov/DHS/ph/pas/faqs.shtml#whatis>.

Orwell, George 1984. June 27, 2006. <http://www.online-literature.com/booksearch.php>.

Palast, Greg "Hugo Chávez." July 2006. The Progressive. May, 19 2007 <http://www.progressive.org/mag_intv0706>.

PBS. "Streamliners Timeline" American Experience. Sept. 13, 2006 <http://www.pbs.org/wgbh/amex/streamliners/timeline/>.

Park, Edwin, Melanie Nathanson, Robert Greenstein, and John Springer. "The Troubling Medicare Legislation." December 8, 2003. Center on Budget and Policy Priorities. July 3, 2007 <http://www.cbpp.org/11-18-03health2.htm>.

People for the American Way. "Civil Rights, Equal Rights: Hostile Climate." Nov 3, 2006 <http://www.pfaw.org/pfaw/general/default.aspx?oid=4139>.

Pipes, Richard. "The Fall of Communism: The Last Empire." 2000. Hoover Digest: Research and Opinion on Public Policy Issue 2000 No. 1. May 9, 2007 <http://www.hoover.org/publications/digest/3476851.html>.

POAC. "Transcripts: Project for the old American Century / White Rose Society message boards Alan Colmes Fox News Radio Neal Horsley Audio." December 11, 2006 <http://oldamericancentury.com/med_may.htm>.

Price, R.G. "The Rise of American Fascism." May 15, 2004. Rational Revolution Online. March 23, 2007 <http://www.rationalrevolution.net/articles/rise_of_american_fascism.htm>.

Public Citizen's Watch. "Pharmaceuticals Rank as Most Profitable Industry, Again: 'Druggernaut' Tops All Three Measures of Profits In New Fortune 500 Report". April 17, 2002. Congress Watch. June 4, 2007 <http://www.citizen.org/documents/fortune500_2002erport.PDF>.

Reclaimdemocracy.org. "Our Hidden History of Corporations in the United States." February 2000. Reclaimdemocracy.org: Restoring Citizen Authority Over Corporations. Novemeber 11, 2006 <http://reclaimdemocracy.org/corporate_accountability/history_corporations_us.html>.

Rector, Robert E. and Kirk Johnson, PhD. "Understanding Poverty in America." September 15, 2004. Heritage Foundation. Novermebr 16, 2006 <http://www.heritage.org/Research/Welfare/bg1796.cfm>.

Robin, Corey. Fear: The History of a Political Idea. New York: Oxford University Press, 2004.

Roland, Allen L. "14 CHARACTERISTICS OF FASCISM: WE HAVE THEM ALL." Sept. 18, 2006. Salon.com. Sept. 22, 2006 <http://blogs.salon.com/0002255/2006/08/31.html#a1397>.

Scheer, Robert. "Gingrich: Do as I Say, Not as I Do." August 17, 1999. Los Angeles Times. January 14, 2007
<http://www.robertscheer.com/1_natcolumn/99_columns/081799.htm>.

Schneider, Greg. "Lockheed's star war is dud so far:Anti-missile missile hasn't hit a thing in four expensive tests; It may lose program to rival; Firm's reputation is on the line in bid for even larger program." Sept. 19, 1998. The Baltimore Sun. December 14, 2006
<http://www.fas.org/spp/starwars/program/news98/980419-lsi.htm>.

School of Americas Watch. "What is the SOA." 2001. School of Americas Watch. September 23, 2006. <http://www.soaw.org/new/type.php?type=8)>.

Spatz, Diana. "Bush Welfare Agenda - Married to a Myth." February, 25 2004. Commondreams. October, 22 2006
<http://www.commondreams.org/views04/0225-11.htm>.

Stinnett, Robert B. "Pearl Harbor: Official Lies in an American War Tragedy?" May 24, 2000. The Independent Institute. October 8, 2006
<http://www.apfn.org/apfn/pearl_harbor.htm>.

Taxpayers for Common Sense. "Contract Value for Reconstructing New Orleans: $254,705,234 through FEMA." Taxpayers for Common Sense. January 16, 2007
<http://www.taxpayer.net/budget/katrinaspending/contracts/bechtel.htm>.

The Nation Magazine. "Barbara Bush: It's Good Enough for the Poor." 2005. January 29, 2006
<http://www.thenation.com/blogs/thebeat?bid=1&pid=20080>.

United States Census Bureau. 2000 "Census."
<http://censtats.census.gov/data/US/01000.pdf>.

United States Department of Labor. "Tax Credit Programs: General Program Information." January 11, 2007
<http://www.doleta.gov/programs/wotcdata.cfm>.

United States Government. "Budget of the United States Government: Browse Fiscal Year 2007." Department of Defence. February, 19 2007
<http://www.gpoaccess.gov/usbudget/fy07/pdf/budget/defense.pdf >.

United States Government Budget. 2007. Department of Defense. March 10, 2007. <http://www.gpoaccess.gov/usbudget/fy07/pdf/budget/defense.pdf

Us.gov 1. "Transcript of Sherman Anti-Trust Act (1890)." 2006. September, 13 2007
<http://www.ourdocuments.gov/doc.php?flash=true&doc=51&page=transcript>.

US.gov 2. 2007. "Terror Alert System." September 29, 2007
<http://www.nationalterroralert.com/>.

Wallace-Wells, Benjamin Mourning "Has Broken: How Bush privatized September 11." October 2003. January 2007

<http://www.washingtonmonthly.com/features/2003/0310.wallace-wells2.html>.

Wallis, Jim. God's Politics: Why the Right Gets It Wrong and the Left Doesn't Get It. New York, New York: Harper Collins, 2005.

WhiteHouse.gov. 2006. September, 4 2006 <http://www.whitehouse.gov/omb/budget/fy2006/hhs.html>.

Whitehurst, Dr. Teresa. December 28, 2004. CommonDreams.org. August, 1 2006 <http://www.commondreams.org/views04/1228-32.htm>.

Williams, Dr. Walter. "Poverty in America." February 19, 2003. Townhall.com. September, 5 2006 <http://www.gmu.edu/departments/economics/wew/articles/03/povamerica.html>.

Zegart, Dan. "Tort 'Reform' Triumphs." 2005. The Nation. August 13, 2007 <http://www.thenation.com/doc/20050307/zegart>.

Zepezauer, Mark. Boomerang: How Our Covert Wars Have Created Enemies Across the Middle East and Brought Terror to America. Monroe, Maine: Common Courage Press. 2003.

Zepezauer, Mark and Arthur Naiman. "Military Waste & Fraud: $172 billion/year." Third World Traveler. 1996. From the book Take the Rich Off Welfare. Odonian Press: Emeryville, CA, 1996.

Zinn, Howard. A People's History of the United States. New York: Harper Collins, 1980.